# John Gary Anderson
### and his
# Maverick Motor Company

# John Gary Anderson
## and his
# Maverick Motor Company

## The Rise and Fall of Henry Ford's
## Rock Hill Rival

### J. Edward Lee

Charleston · London

History
PRESS

Published by The History Press
Charleston, SC 29403
www.historypress.net

*Cover images: Top:* Two of John Gary Anderson's grandsons, John Anderson Hardin and John Anderson Gill, proudly display their vintage automobiles on the campus of Winthrop University in 1965. *Bottom:* A 1922 Anderson Car, flanked by close-up photographs, parked on a snowy day in front of the stately Anderson home on Rock Hill's Oakland Avenue.

First published 2007

Manufactured in the United Kingdom

ISBN 978.1.59629.229.1

Library of Congress Cataloging-in-Publication Data

Lee, J. Edward, 1953-
   John Gary Anderson and his maverick motor company The rise and fall of Henry Fords Rock Hill Rival / J. Edward Lee.
      p. cm.
   Includes bibliographical references.
   ISBN 978-1-59629-229-1 (alk. paper)
   1. Anderson, John Gary, 1861-1937. 2. Businessmen--United
States--Biography. 3. Anderson Motor Company (Rock Hill, S.C.)--History. 4.
Automobile industry and trade--United States--History. I. Title.
   HD9710.U52A55 2007
   338.7'629222092--dc22
   [B]
                          2006100261

For my parents
Tyre Douglas Lee Sr. (1905–1992)
Ola Bankhead Lee (1911–1981)

# Contents

John Gary Anderson proudly promoted his automobiles throughout the region. This 1920 Anderson Touring Car is posed at Charleston, South Carolina's Colonial Lake.

# Acknowledgements

I learned early in my career the pivotal role archivists and librarians can play in guiding research projects such as *John Gary Anderson and his Maverick Motor Company: The Rise and Fall of Henry Ford's Rock Hill Rival.* Retired Winthrop University archivist Ron Chepesiuk, one of my mentors, knew the holdings of his repository like the back of his hand. Ron unlocked the treasures of his facility for my inspection and shared his considerable wisdom. His successor, Gina Price White, similarly aided my search for the impact visionaries like John Gary Anderson have upon their towns. David Lyon, the director of the York County Library, has assembled a courteous and helpful staff, and these librarians gave me ready access to the main library's Caroliniana Room. Great Falls Public Library Director Lea G. Grant, who single-handedly built her library's local history room from scratch, encouraged me to complete this project, assisting me every step of the way as I (a child of the 1950s) tried to master modern technology, one of her specialties.

Three of John Gary Anderson's grandsons—James C. Hardin Jr., John A. Hardin and John A. Gill—gave me honorary membership in the extraordinary Anderson family. They knew the automaker, who they called "Other Poppa," as a loving patriarch, and these men helped me gain valuable insights into the man who grandson James Hardin called "hungry." More on these men in the introduction.

Great-grandson Walter Anderson Hardin, Jim's son, clearly explained the demise of the company and the defective Continental engines that contributed to the death of the Anderson Car. This malfunction, Walter stressed, damaged not just the 1924 model but also wrecked the company's reputation at a crucial moment. The whispers of "engine problems" quickly became shouts of doubt.

In the South, personal contacts are to be cultivated. My mother-in-law, Jacqueline Allen Hardy, the granddaughter of one of Anderson's Rock Hill contemporaries, former Mayor John J. Waters, helped me understand how transplants like Waters and Anderson fell in love with Rock Hill. William C. Beatty Jr., an executive with Comporium Communications and a descendant of James Milton Cherry, provided me access to some of Cherry's business records. Cherry, the so-called Alfalfa King and former Anderson partner, shared John Gary Anderson's zeal for a diversified economy. Partners such as Cherry helped Anderson scramble up the economic ladder in his adopted hometown.

Carol Hanlon, the administrative assistant for Winthrop University's history department, cheerfully turned my handwritten manuscript into neatly typed prose. Carol has done this for me before, and I appreciate her enthusiasm for telling the story of the Anderson Car.

At The History Press, the editors, Jenny Kaemmerlen and Deborah Carver, shaped the manuscript and turned it into a beautiful testament to John Gary Anderson's work ethic and his impact on Rock Hill. They are lovers of the written word, of books, and I hope to partner with them again because The History Press is a recognized leader in local and regional history.

Ann Hardy Lee, my wife, and Elizabeth Ann Lee, my daughter, always encourage me. They, like the folks at The History Press, love books and they love me. Elizabeth demonstrated her commitment to *John Gary Anderson* by preparing the final draft for the editors.

# Introduction

*You can do anything you want to.*
*Inscription from John Gary Anderson to grandson*
*James C. Hardin, Jr. in* Autobiography

While researching *John Gary Anderson and his Maverick Motor Company*, I had the pleasure of interviewing three of John Gary Anderson's grandsons. By the dawn of the twenty-first century, all three of these men were senior adults. All of them had been successful businessmen in Rock Hill, South Carolina, the site of the Anderson Automobile Company. They, like the family patriarch, had left their mark on this New South city.

The youngest, John Anderson Gill, was boisterous and physically active. Born in 1932, "Johnny" Gill, was only five years of age when his famous grandfather succumbed. He hazily remembered crawling under the entrepreneur's feet on the family's front porch. Even after the demise of the Anderson Company, visitors would make respectful pilgrimages to the Queen Anne–style home, seeking advice and reliving the brief moment when the Anderson Car gave Henry Ford a competitive race. As a child, Johnny Gill grasped the fact that the automaker was a leader, respected for his accomplishments. He vaguely recalls "Other Poppa," but he knew the widow Anderson, "Other Mama," who lived until 1959, much better. Gill owned an independent insurance agency, its office located in the shadow of the historic Anderson home. Gill lovingly returned the home to its past grandeur, restoring the stately dwelling on Rock Hill's Oakland Avenue, near the Winthrop University campus.[1]

Gill had spent adulthood immersed, like his grandfather, in civic affairs. Any activity of the chamber of commerce, any city festival, any Winthrop

In 1898 the thirty-seven-year-old John Gary Anderson, confident and ambitious as a new century dawned, posed for this portrait.

sporting event could always count on Johnny Gill. When the town began its annual "Come See Me" spring festival in the 1960s, Gill enlisted in the cause. When Winthrop's baseball team pursued the College World Series, Gill cheered from the bleachers, wearing a burgundy cap with the letter "W" emblazoned on it.[2]

A second grandson, John Anderson Hardin, excelled as a leader locally, regionally and nationally as a savings and loan president. As his grandfather before him, he traveled across the country promoting the National Savings and Loan League, an organization over which he presided. His influence in shaping modern Rock Hill is well documented. The city of nearly sixty thousand residents is built on a financial foundation made possible by Hardin's loans to homeowners and businesses. Born in 1920, John Hardin knew his grandfather well and inherited an affection for the New South, with all of its potential and capital needs. As a young banking executive, John Hardin served as the city's mayor while also lobbying national leaders on behalf of his All-America City (so designated in 1969), as well as promoting the interests of savings and loan institutions. His trademark rainbow-hued sports coats (with lush greens and dazzling purples) remind one of John Gary Anderson's cars: eye-catching and attention-grabbing. Businesspeople must boldly advertise their products, loudly calling attention to themselves. John Gary Anderson mastered that essential marketing tactic. "Nothing could be finer" than his gorgeous automobiles that outshined the drab, but cheaper, Fords.[3]

James "Jim" Carlisle Hardin Jr., however, knew John Gary Anderson best. Born in 1915, Jim Hardin caddied for his grandfather, chauffeured him around town, drove him to his Florida home in exile and listened to his stories of success—and failure. The latter were often bitterly directed at bankers who, in the company's hour of need, walked away from the stranded Anderson Car. They turned their backs on the man who had worked so hard to build a New South city, and they became seduced by outsiders. Jim Hardin, cerebral and sophisticated, was an engineer by the time his grandfather passed away, and it would be Hardin who picked up the remnants of the Anderson Company and reassembled them as Rock Hill Body Company, managing that firm until the early 1980s.[4]

Sitting with octogenarian Jim Hardin in his spacious Lake Wylie, South Carolina home, I grasped the essence of John Gary Anderson, who Hardin called "a hell of a smart man and a nice man." While Jim was a Duke University–trained engineer, the automaker was self-taught but "a smart man," nonetheless.[5] The patriarch understood the power of the vehicle that would propel America to world leadership. He was, in a sense, a fearless pioneer, moving an infant industry forward and waging a war he would lose with Detroit's Henry Ford.

To John Gary Anderson, a well-designed well-made, well-marketed car would speed to the head of the pack, leaving the bewildered competition in its dust. But, as we shall see and as Jim Hardin and I discussed on that February afternoon, by the late 1920s, the genius of this bold entrepreneur would be wrecked by the cheaper Ford, chronic engine defects and exhausted capital. Still, John Gary Anderson's story is the uplifting saga of the New South, which emerged from the ashes of the Civil War. It is a chronicle boldly written by a risk-taker who Jim Hardin recalled as "a hungry visionary."[6]

# Hungry Visionary

*Mr. Anderson was the typical successful American businessman of the past half century. He was entirely self-made, having had little schooling and no financial start in life.*
Rock Hill Evening Herald, *December 16, 1937*

John Gary Anderson, born in the first year of the Civil War on November 27, 1861, lived for more than three-quarters of a century. During his lifetime, he witnessed the wreckage left behind by the war, the chaotic attempts at Reconstruction, lingering racism, the rebuilding of a shattered Southern economy, the reordering of society, landmark political change, the dilemma of uneven cotton prices and the dawn of significant industrialization—including his automobile company as well as that of Henry Ford.[1]

John Gary Anderson lived amid all of these developments and their distinctive challenges. Anderson's life stretched from the Old South to nearly the middle of the twentieth century. It was an extraordinary time to be alive, and one could not help but accept the waves of change that swept across the South from 1861 until Anderson's death in 1937. And Anderson swam at the zenith of the crest, often alone. To understand John Gary Anderson fully, one must return to 1861, the time of his birth.[2]

The Old South, with its narrow ruling oligarchy and its peculiar institutions, was doomed even before shots were fired on Fort Sumter in April 1861. It was a land whose sins were chronicled in the pages of William Lloyd Garrison's newspaper, *The Liberator*. Harriet Beecher Stowe, in her classic 1852 novel *Uncle Tom's Cabin*, wrote passionately about a system of human bondage that stained every Southerner, white and black. Slavery sapped the vitality of the cotton kingdom and eroded the moral

This collage features the "hungry visionary" from childhood (upper left) to middle age (center).

foundation of the region. The South was a tightly wound society with an irrational, flawed justification for its peculiarities. Cotton may be king, as South Carolina's James Henry Hammond boasted on the floor of the U.S. Senate in 1858, but the crop would strangle the region. By December 1860, when South Carolina, angry that its fugitive slaves were not pursued by the federal government, seceded from the Union, the outcome of the pending conflict should have been apparent: the economically superior North, with its industries, banks, railroads and larger population would overwhelm the Rebels. A weak Confederacy, with its decentralization, would be handicapped by political squabbles and states' rights. Battlefield defeats would accumulate until, in the autumn of 1864, William Tecumseh Sherman sliced his way across Georgia and, by early 1865, into the proud Carolinas. The Union general's March to the Sea was total war, and it traumatized the Confederacy, dismantling the social order, disrupting the economy and exposing the flaws that had disguised themselves from the jubilant secessionists of a few years earlier. The land would be trampled, bathed in blood, splattering a generation of citizens.[3]

John Gary Anderson was a member of this generation. Born on November 27, 1861, in Lawsonville, North Carolina, Anderson was briefly tied to the Old South, dominated by the precious cotton and the forced labor required to cultivate that crop. Within eighteen months, however, the Confederacy had lost the talented General Thomas Jonathan "Stonewall" Jackson (at the May 1863 battle of Chancellorsville) and suffered simultaneous defeats that July at Gettysburg and Vicksburg. The latter battle split the South into two parts, separated by the Mississippi River. There would be no independence. There would be no foreign recognition. There would be no agricultural paradise. The tide was receding. Rather, there would be a wide swath of charred land stretching from Atlanta to Raleigh. Columbia, the citadel of the Deep South, was laid to waste by an inferno that could be seen fifty miles away.[4]

Thus, John Gary Anderson was born during the worst of times. There were no "best of times." His early years—spent in Lawsonville and with relatives in Landsford along South Carolina's Catawba River—coincided with the death of the Old South. Before he was four years of age, his homeland had collapsed amid its cotton, smothered by the North's industrial might, strangled by Union generals like Ulysses S. Grant and Sherman. Its leaders had become discredited (James Longstreet at Gettysburg) or were dead (Jackson and J.E.B. Stuart). Even the great commander Robert E. Lee had become militarily impotent, surrendering to Grant in April 1865 at Appomattox Court House.[5]

Anderson was, as his grandson James C. Hardin Jr. succinctly explained, "hungry." It was—in the tumultuous 1860s—impossible to be otherwise in

One year before his death, Anderson reflected on his life of lofty successes and crushing failures.

the Southland. Among the parched fields of the dying Old South, hunger was literal, figurative and psychological. This hunger motivated the young boy, creating in him an insatiable drive to succeed. It would remain with him all of his life. He was determined, even as a child, to rise from the ashes of the discredited Old South and lead the way to something better. His childhood poverty, his modest three and one half months of formal schooling, the deaths of both parents as the result of tuberculosis, the utter dissolution of the South—none of these obstacles would derail his ambition. He was a hungry visionary, realizing that intelligence comes from more than a classroom experience. Success, hard work and bold dreams are interwoven. And in 1880 John Gary Anderson, not yet out of his teens, would arrive in the railroad village of Rock Hill, South Carolina, with visions—dreams—of contributing to a New South.[6]

For more than fifty years, John Gary Anderson enthusiastically shared and promoted his visions. He participated in Rock Hill's economic rise by playing a leading role in establishing a chamber of commerce, newspaper, telephone company, electrification, a progressive approach to cotton pricing, the growth of a college and the buggy business that evolved, by the early twentieth century, into a manufacturer of automobiles. The Anderson Car, with its rich colors and luxurious design, was his most noteworthy achievement, but it was far from his only contribution to constructing a New South. In 1937, when the visionary was laid to rest on a knoll within sight of the factory that had once produced nearly six thousand Anderson automobiles, those assembled mourners pondered the times that had created such a driven man, the hunger that motivated him.[7]

# Death of a Salesman

*As much as any other citizen he contributed to the upbuilding of Rock Hill through his own enterprises and through his encouragement of the textile industry and his efforts in understanding of a purely civil nature.*
Rock Hill Evening Herald, *December 16, 1937*

A week before Christmas 1937, John Gary Anderson, the hungry visionary, died in exile of a heart attack after playing nine holes of golf. After the collapse of his South Carolina automobile manufacturing company in 1926, he spent much of his time playing golf in Lakeland, Florida. He maintained a stately Queen Anne–style home in Rock Hill, the site of his failed automobile company, but he had turned his attention and vision southward when Rock Hill abandoned him and his car. Florida would be the South's new frontier and it became his winter refuge. But, until his demise, he remained a competitor, using his prowess to evade sand traps and water hazards and to navigate fairways. Anderson, the driven salesman who had risen from the debris of war and marketed the finely crafted luxurious automobiles that bore his name, now walked around the Lakeland links, accompanied by his grandson James C. Hardin Jr., who served as his reliable caddy. Anderson, ill from the battles that had inflicted their wounds upon him, reflected upon the changes that had occurred in the South and in his life during his seventy-six years.[1]

At his funeral, it was stressed, there were certain things that had remained constant in John Gary Anderson's long life—even as change swirled about him. He cherished Alice Louetta Holler Anderson and his six children: Genevieve Louetta, John Wesley, Mary Christine, Carrie, William Adlai and Alice Ellwood. Orphaned at an early age, John Gary

After the collapse of his enterprise, Anderson and his wife, Alice Louetta Holler Anderson, spent much time at their Lakeland, Florida home. This photograph was taken in 1935, two years before the automaker's death.

Anderson clung tenaciously to his large family and lived long enough to see the rise of a second generation—James Hardin and his cousins, who called their grandfather "Other Poppa." Alice would be "Other Mama." The grandsons would be enlisted as active pallbearers for the patriarch.[2] In this solid personal life there was no hint of scandal, no philandering or abuse. His family came first, and that's why he salvaged the homes—in Rock Hill and Lakeland—from the wreckage of his financial troubles. The Rock Hill house would be the site of his funeral. His family was first class and they lived in impressive homes that demonstrated Anderson's success. His widow, Alice Holler Anderson, deserved as much because her father and her brother had believed in the young Anderson, taking the hungry visionary into the buggy business and nudging him toward the automobile.[3]

They were a sober clan, all teetotalers. At the turn of the twentieth century in 1901, Anderson had helped found a Rock Hill newspaper, the *Journal*, which was a "dry" publication. In his personal conduct, Anderson was an unbending prohibitionist. Alcohol undermined society, Anderson reasoned, and diluted productivity. As a teetotaling Methodist, he was disciplined in his crusade, in print and in words, against liquor.[4]

Anderson saw links between his family, his religion, his moral values and his business initiatives. A "dry" newspaper strengthened the community, educating the workforce about the perils of alcohol. Rock Hill (and the Anderson offspring) must be protected from the enemy if there was to be progress—and Anderson knew that there must be steady progress, always.[5]

The large crowd, which assembled in Rock Hill's Laurelwood Cemetery on the cloudy afternoon of December 19, 1937, noted John Gary Anderson's commitment to the town's chamber of commerce, telephone company, electrification, college, banks, buggies and automobiles. The salesman had displayed a wide-ranging commitment to building a New South, inhabited by energetic, sober, educated, hardworking people. He refused to let his modest upbringing restrict him; being born during the Civil War became a blessing rather than a handicap. It forced him to educate himself, form alliances (with educators like Winthrop College founder David Bancroft Johnson and businessman James Milton Cherry), imagine new solutions to old problems and market his vision far beyond one small city. Today, we would say that he thought outside the box.

By the time of his death, John Gary Anderson had seen some of his dreams become commonplace and accepted. For instance, Franklin D. Roosevelt was piercing the darkness with his Rural Electrification Administration. And New South businesspeople, including James Buchanan Duke, were damming the region's waterways and creating electricity to light every hamlet along the Catawba River. Duke and FDR, like Anderson, understood the partnerships that could energize an area that, a few decades earlier, had been destitute. Even the Tennessee Valley was being reborn as its river system was harnessed for the public good.[6]

In 1911 Anderson lamented the irony that farmers who succeeded in mastering the land could, when they overproduced cotton, fall victim to low prices despite the sweat of their brows. Early in the twentieth century, Anderson had devised a strategy for boosting cotton prices. Anderson's Rock Hill Plan encouraged reduced production while increasing the prices paid to farmers. With money in their pockets, these tillers of the soil could ride their wagons to Rock Hill and, perhaps, purchase automobiles. Roosevelt's agricultural policies similarly sought to raise cotton prices, regulate acreage, reduce production and give farmers more money to purchase durable goods—like fancy automobiles. Everyone would prosper.

The salesman had, in many ways, been ahead of his time. But he had taken the cards dealt him, as tattered as they were, patched them, reconfigured them, dusted them off, shined them and ably played them to their utmost utility. And the crowd gathered in Laurelwood Cemetery recognized, on that December afternoon, that John Gary Anderson had taught Detroit's Henry Ford—and the bankers who abandoned the Anderson Car—something about the strength of a man of the New South. "Defeat" and "failure" were not part of his vocabulary, and they were far from the minds of the grieving throng that watched John Gary Anderson laid to rest in Laurelwood, in a plot within sight of the Anderson Company factory, an enduring symbol of the dreams of the New South he had championed.[7]

# Music to His Ears

*My grandfather never forgot where he came from.*
*James C. Hardin Jr.*

Lawsonville, North Carolina, in 1861 was a community of a few hundred whites and their slaves who cultivated the land. In his nearly nine-hundred-page autobiography, a comprehensive review of his life completed shortly before his death, John Gary Anderson writes that the whites "lived in regal splendor." The town was named for Bobbie Lawson, a bachelor who presided over this agricultural paradise. "Uncle Bobbie," as Anderson called him, was a member of the antebellum Southern aristocracy. There were rumors that Uncle Bobbie's colonial mansion, located across the road from Anderson's grandparents' house, rested on a fortune of buried gold. The young Anderson dreamed of retrieving some of this mysterious treasure, outfitting himself in finery and journeying to the circus to watch the animals and acrobats. When Uncle Bobbie died in the 1870s, however, a brother inherited the estate and there was no sign of the gold. In his autobiography, Anderson confides, "I later examined the hearth carefully to see if it had been tampered with, but could see no signs of molestation. I don't suppose Uncle Bobbie's brother knew the gold was there." The South, with its small elite of slave owners benefiting from the fruit of forced labor, was built symbolically on similar fantasies. And, with the defeat of the cotton kingdom, the fortune had vanished.[1]

Uncle Bobbie's colonial mansion survived the war, but Lawsonville deteriorated. With the social order transformed by the end of slavery, the citizens of Lawsonville migrated to a newer town, Reidsville, where they opened businesses. The war had so altered the landscape—literally—that

Upon his arrival in Rock Hill, Anderson entered into a partnership with Adlai Holler, married the boss's daughter and formed a number of friendships with businesspeople who were shaping the New South city.

Old South hamlets like Lawsonville ceased to exist. Reidsville, like John Gary Anderson's future home of Rock Hill in South Carolina, would be saved by the railroad. In Reidsville's case, it was the Richmond-Danville line and the town's future would be bright. Lawsonville's destiny was handicapped by its addiction to slave labor and agriculture. The New South's future had room for neither. Even as a small child, witnessing this change as it swirled about him, Anderson seems to have glimpsed the future of his region. In fact, his grandfather, John H. Thomas, contrasted with Uncle Bobbie and influenced John Gary Anderson's career decisions. Thomas would be a New South man while Uncle Bobbie was a member of the Old South gentry.[2]

Thomas lived across from Lawson's plantation. While Uncle Bobbie tied himself to the land, John Thomas owned just twenty acres and, Anderson recalls, "did not pretend to farm." Rather, his grandfather manufactured, with slave labor, carriages and wagons, making $50,000 in Confederate money during the war. The business produced one hundred of these wagons a year for the Lost Cause, fulfilling its commitment to supply vehicles for that doomed effort. Everything was made "by hand," including nails and chains. These were covered wagons, beautifully crafted. Anderson notes, "The whole thing was fascinating to me. I just loved to be around and hear the bellows roar and the anvils ring. It was music to my ears." Thus, Anderson's fascination with vehicles began early. The laborers, white and black, were strong and impressive. Anderson's grandfather seemed to be a giant of a man, "not to be trifled with." Grandfather Thomas was, Anderson observed, "full of energy and enthusiasm." More was needed to succeed, and by 1865 Uncle Bobbie's gold coins and John Thomas's wagon business were swept away by the South's military defeat.[3]

Confederate contracts meant nothing—neither did the piles of currency accumulating in Thomas's carriage business. The Rebel money proclaimed it would have value after a treaty of peace between the North and the South, but there would be no "treaty of peace" or recognition of the Confederacy's legitimacy. Robert E. Lee's surrender at Appomattox Court House and the Union occupation of the Southland left Thomas penniless and the family destitute. Gone were the plentiful hams, chickens, cows—and the African American laborers. The first years of the new social order was especially painful for the young Anderson. What had gone wrong? Had his grandfather not worked hard enough? Were not the wagons finely crafted? Had the business not fulfilled its obligation to the Confederacy? Despite these troubles, Anderson matured early, helping his grandfather squeeze food from the property. He wrote, "You can do a lot of things that are 'impossible' when there is no other alternative." His grandfather, with the wagon business defunct, remained "a man of energy and initiative and no problem could faze him."[4] Life's ravines could not trap a man of vision.

During the war, Anderson's parents had journeyed from time to time to his paternal family's home in Landsford, South Carolina. Landsford was an ancient shallow crossing on the Catawba River. During the American Revolution, Patriots like William Richardson Davie, the founder of the University of North Carolina, had lived there and the land was sprinkled with the blood of Whigs who had fought Great Britain's Banastre Tarleton and Christian Huck, winning the battle for independence. A canal had been constructed by Irish workers in 1823. The Landsford Canal was supposed to be part of a network of canals that would stretch from Charleston to Cincinnati, bypassing the churning waterfalls of rivers like the Catawba. Anderson knew this history and he knew that the Landsford Canal would never be profitable because the railroad came and eclipsed it as a means of transportation. At Landsford, Anderson learned about history, technology and the power of ideas. His family ran a mill on the Catawba River, harnessing a portion of the river to grind grain into meal. In his autobiography, he stressed that the river could be tamed, directed, channeled by human beings who boldly saw "the tremendous potential value of the water running down the Catawba Valley from the mountains to the sea." Most people, Anderson stressed, did not have the vision to contemplate such ventures as river-generated electricity. He estimated that only five in fifteen thousand think of such things. It was that small but talented group who would, Anderson observed, "blaze a new trail," and he yearned for membership in that elite fraternity.[5] The seeds of ambition were planted in the young boy's fertile mind.

Because of the war's disruption, Anderson spent only a few months in the classroom. In his autobiography, he claimed that he remembered little of his formal education. Compounding his bleak situation was the death of his father—"everyone liked him"—in 1867 at age twenty-nine. Three years later, Anderson's mother—"my best friend"—would also succumb to tuberculosis. John Gary Anderson, at age nine, and his baby sister, Jet, were left to the care of their grandparents Thomas. Philosophically, Anderson tells us, "If one really wants to know how to appreciate good times, imagine one's self in my shoes in the early Seventies, Grandpa, my only protector, past seventy, and me, a little boy without experience, having to begin the battles of life, under the circumstances and conditions that then prevailed throughout the South."[6] As we shall see, hardships, such as losing both parents, would never deter Anderson. Adversity always seemed to strengthen him.

Even as a boy of ten, Anderson saw himself in the minority of visionaries who were not content to meekly bow their heads and accept their lots in life. He was one of the visionaries; he had seen the Confederate wagons that his grandfather had manufactured during the Civil War; they had produced "music to his ears." And, despite the fact that the war had ended in a crushing defeat for the South, John Gary Anderson, parentless, was hungry but far from vanquished. He just needed to find a New South town where he could allow his vision to take root and produce nourishment.

# They Call It Rock Hill

*Goodness knows I'm glad Rock Hill never "evolved" into the typical*
*Southern court house town, populated by a horde of little lawyers*
*and county politicians and checker players.*
John Gary Anderson, *Autobiography*

As noted earlier, Landsford, South Carolina, is a hamlet located on the Catawba River, a waterway that slices through the Piedmont regions of both Carolinas. Named for an early settler, Thomas Land, the community has deep historical roots. During the American Revolution, Patriots and Loyalists skirmished nearby, especially in 1780 as the battle of Kings Mountain loomed. Along the Catawba's banks, Patriots were soundly defeated at the battle of Fishing Creek in the summer of 1780; their commander, Thomas Sumter, was forced to flee hastily northward.[1]

By the time John Gary Anderson arrived at Landsford, however, the War of Independence had been won. The site was known for a more recent historical event. Around 1820, bold entrepreneurs, including architect Robert Mills, envisioned an elaborate system of canals, which would wind their way through the Lowcountry of South Carolina into the Midlands, slicing through the Piedmont. This canal network would, its promoters believed, transport cotton and other agricultural products from South Carolina to, ultimately, the Midwest markets.[2]

Irish immigrant workers tediously constructed the Landsford section of the system. Blocks of granite were carved, moved through the woods, laid atop each other and ultimately diverted the Catawba River in a bypass around rough shoals. The Landsford Canal was completed, at a cost of $123,000 in 1823. Then, in a lesson to all who dream about fortunes and acclaim, the canal was eclipsed by the advent of the railroad, a new technological feat that could move cotton faster and cheaper to Ohio. The Landsford Canal was abandoned, never making a profit. But, in the 1860s as now, it stood as a monument to man's courageous (but painstaking) efforts to triumph economically if only he could reach high and fast enough. That lesson of dreams, sweat and risks—and the harsh uncertainty of ever-evolving technology—would impact the life of John Gary Anderson.

At Landsford, the young John Gary Anderson had seen the remains of the canal, which was supposed to facilitate transportation of cotton bales from the coastal city of Charleston to the interior of the United States all the way to Cincinnati, Ohio—bringing riches to South Carolina planters. Despite a Robert Mills design and the sweat of Irish workers, the Landsford Canal never fulfilled its mission. Instead, the railroad swept past it, moving people and goods across the South and into the nation's interior. The railroad was a giant step forward and it bypassed towns like Lawsonville and gave birth to new villages like Reidsville and Rock Hill.[3]

John Roddey, a surveyor for the railroad, recorded his impression of the community in which Anderson would manufacture his automobile. Poking through the flint in 1852, on a small rise Roddey observed, "They call it Rock Hill." The town, however, did not really exist in 1852. Other cities, such as Yorkville, Chesterville and Winnsboro, far outdistanced it. These three places were historic courthouse towns and had been such for more than fifty years. In Yorkville, the Confederacy's President Jefferson Davis spent a night in the fine home of Dr. J. Rufus Bratton, near the beautiful Rose Hotel that had been built the same year John Roddey was shoveling through the rocky soil of Rock Hill, as the South collapsed in 1865.[4] Mary Boykin Chesnut, the Civil War diarist, spent the conflict's last weeks in Chesterville, in a modest rented room, recording her thoughts about the defeat of her beloved homeland. And Winnsboro had been headquarters for Lord Charles Cornwallis in the earlier conflict of the American Revolution. The Union villain Sherman brushed against Winnsboro brutally during his March to the Sea. These three cities, as well as nearby Lancaster, were well established by the mid-nineteenth century. They were, in every way, Old South.

In York County, places like Ebenezerville, with its private academy and thriving Associate Reformed Presbyterian Church, were much more prominent than Rock Hill, which was in 1860—in the words of one historian—"a smokey place." Smoky, sparsely populated and built on land that had been snatched from the Catawba, at the outbreak of the Civil War, Rock Hill only had one hundred residents. The war, as we have seen, changed much about the area. And the coming of the locomotive would change even more. In 1851 when Ebenezerville refused the Charlotte-

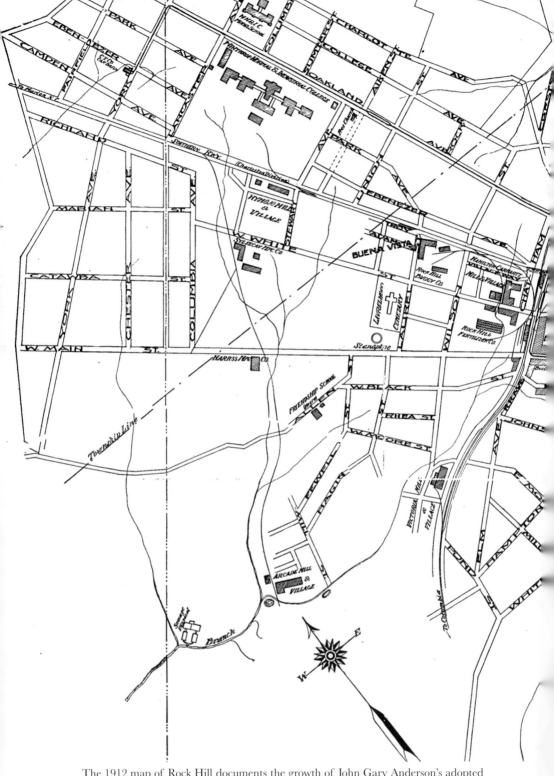

The 1912 map of Rock Hill documents the growth of John Gary Anderson's adopted hometown. His buggy company can be found on the left, nestled between Laurel and Wilson Streets.

"ROCK HILL IS A GOOD TOWN"

~ MAP ~
~ OF ~
Rock Hill
~ S·C· ~
1912

ARCHITECT ~ N GAILLARD WALKER ~ ENGINEER

Columbia-Augusta Railroad a right of way, Rock Hill, which may have been smoky but certainly was not slow, pounced. Landowner John Templeton Black donated four acres to lure the railroad. That gift brought surveyor Roddey to the hill that gave the community its name.[5] Rock Hill welcomed prizes—and ideas—that other cities rejected.

The Civil War brushed against Rock Hill. Jefferson Davis, during his long surrender in April 1865, rode hurriedly past the town, heading for Dr. Rufus Bratton's home in Yorkville. Retreating Confederates crossed the Catawba River at Nation Ford but they, like their president, did not tarry in small Rock Hill. Thus, Rock Hill escaped the destruction of other cities like Columbia and Atlanta from Sherman's March, which swept to the east of the Catawba River. The town was inconsequential, overlooked and of no strategic value to the Union military. But John Gary Anderson noticed it.

In his autobiography, Anderson writes about his first impressions of Rock Hill during the war years. As a young child, barely a toddler, he traveled through Rock Hill on his way from Lawsonville, where his maternal grandparents lived, to the mill at Landsford that was ran by his Anderson kin. He wrote that the village was originally called "Rocky Hill" because of its terrain. To him, that name "sounds foolish and ridiculous," and the town's inhabitants compressed it. By 1868 the railroad was already affecting Rock Hill. Stores and saloons were springing up near the depot and the population had tripled to three hundred people. And new residents, ambitious people with dreams of building a New South city, arrived to make their mark. Natural instincts, vision and hard work—not pedigree or land ownership—opened doors of opportunity in places likes Rock Hill. In 1867 James Morrow Ivy, a Confederate veteran, formed a company at Beatty's Ford, just across the Catawba River in North Carolina. He realized the potential of the railroad town to the New South and in 1870 founded a company in Rock Hill that bought cotton, sold fertilizer and did private banking. Ivy purchased cotton from area farmers, paying more than buyers in Camden and Columbia. Farmers loaded their wagons with their harvest and headed to see Mr. Ivy. In his book *A City Without Cobwebs,* Douglas Summers Brown tells us, "Rock Hill almost became a boom town, growing to the tune of turning wagon wheels carrying the cotton crop to the warehouses."[6] Rock Hill tapped the energy of Southerners who were seeking new markets and better prices.

In his memoirs, Anderson reflected on Ivy's impact upon Rock Hill. The cotton buyer paid top dollar to grateful farmers and, before they boarded their wagons to return to their fields, "what a big pile of money they left with the merchants!" Everyone benefited from Ivy's generosity—including the railroad town, which grew at a rapid rate. Ivy dealt in cotton futures and anticipated crops and helped solidify the link between business and farm. When Ivy died in 1885, one citizen named Ben Fewell lamented, "The light and life of the town died yesterday afternoon at five o'clock...his friends ranged from the beggar to the banker."[7] The town, as we know, would welcome other visionaries, men who would contribute to the town's "light."

Others made their presence known in early Rock Hill. John James Waters, a native of Chester County, came to Rock Hill in 1869 to practice law. Immediately, he became active in Reconstruction politics, assisting Wade Hampton's Red Shirts in redeeming the state in the 1876 gubernatorial election. As Reconstruction ended, Waters helped establish the Rock Hill Hook and Ladder Company to fight fires as well as the town's first public library. Eventually, he would be a councilman (like John Gary Anderson) and mayor.[8]

The post-bellum years witnessed the arrival of William Lyle Roddey in 1866; his family would make their presence known immediately in legal and business circles. The same year Arnold Friedheim, a Jewish merchant, came to Rock Hill and established a thriving department store business not far from the railroad depot. Three years later, businessman John London arrived. And in 1872 James M. Cherry, an ambitious young man from Chester County, arrived as a clerk.[9]

Cherry, like so many of these quick-witted, ambitious men, grasped the potential of the growing town. He would serve with John J. Waters on the fire department organizing committee. By 1888, Cherry was elected, as Waters would be, to the town council, and he eventually became mayor in 1890. Cherry developed real estate, became a partner to John Gary Anderson in the buggy business in 1901 and helped bring electricity to the community the year he was chosen mayor. A decade later, Cherry helped pave the road, which now bears his name, that led to the Catawba River—through land that Cherry developed as growth took hold.[10] Thus, immigrants shaped Rock Hill. The Jewish Friedheim was accepted in the city; his store windows displayed the latest ladies' fashions and his showcases were full of hardware. Waters's law practice flourished and Cherry profitably speculated in real estate.

Anderson made his way to Rock Hill, a town he had passed during the war and a village in which his deceased father had sold tobacco products, in the late 1870s. His life to that point had been painful. As we have seen, both parents had died. Farming in Lawsonville was difficult; sometimes the Thomas family nearly starved during Reconstruction. The autobiography's early pages chronicle a life of deprivation, real hunger and little time for education. Briefly, in 1876, Anderson tried his luck as a printer at the

Reidsville newspaper, but his fortune in that town was no better than it had been on his grandparents' farm in Lawsonville.[11]

At age sixteen, John Gary Anderson, his sister and his grandfather Anderson rode the train down to Rock Hill from Charlotte. Arriving at 11:00 p.m. on a December night in 1877, Anderson recalled the conductor called out, "Rock Hill! All out for Rock Hill!" As the passengers disembarked, Anderson said, "The only place open was a saloon and Grandpa made for it to get a drink and we followed."[12]

Anderson immediately went to work. He performed odd jobs for widows, served as a bartender in one of the town's saloons (and developed a strong antipathy toward alcohol and its effects) and clerked in stores. Basically on his own, as his grandparents died soon after, he scrambled up the ladder that made itself available to him. He became a printer for the local newspaper, the *Herald*, in 1880, and excelled in that business, realizing the power of ideas and words. In Rock Hill, the railroad town that was now John Gary Anderson's home, he prepared to form alliances that would assist him in his climb farther up that ladder.[13]

# Anderson and Company

*Rock Hill almost became a boom town, growing to the tune of
turning wagon wheels carrying the cotton crop to the warehouses.*
Douglas Summers Brown, A City Without Cobwebs

In the Old South families settled in, farmed their land, accepted and
capitalized upon the peculiar institution of slavery, married their
neighbors, worshiped in the same churches and did not dream of bold
initiatives like James Morrow Ivy's cotton market with its generous prices
that filtered down to the merchants of Rock Hill. Ivy's warehouse bulged
with the crops of farmers who favored him—and his fair prices—over the
markets of Old South cities like Columbia or Camden. Those were places
that practiced business as usual—buyers and sellers were often adversaries,
suspicious of each other's intentions. In Rock Hill, Ivy was the farmer's
partner, looking to the future, sharing the wealth with everyone. Similarly,
Cherry looked beyond the gold fields of alfalfa.[1]

The Holler clan, like so many of the other families that built the New
South city of Rock Hill, came from somewhere else. Arriving in Rock Hill
in 1869, Captain Adlai Holler, the family patriarch, was a native of Chester
County, an Old South community settled by the Scotch-Irish who drifted
down the Great Wagon Road from Philadelphia in five waves in the mid-
and late 1700s. They settled in the Carolina Piedmont, naming counties
after Pennsylvania communities: Lancaster, York and Chester. Many of
them were Presbyterian, and they were conservative in their politics, social
mores and economic outlook. They brought with them a reverence for
liberty—for themselves—and a narrow philosophy that left little room for
experimentation. Holler, a non-slaveowner, however, was a Methodist, and

The Rock Hill Buggy Company—like its successor, the Anderson Car Company—
produced stylish vehicles pictured on these pages and pages 40–41.

BUGGY CO.

HILL, S. C.

ROCK HILL BU
ROCK HILL

Y CO.

he was far from narrow in his outlook. The Civil War had changed that—if it had ever existed in the man.[2]

Adlai Holler's military record was impressive. Before the bombardment of Fort Sumter, Holler, a carpenter, had volunteered for the Chester Rifles and had been present in Charleston for the attack on the Union installation. During the war, Holler was wounded three times, including once at the 1864 battle of the Wilderness. He suffered typhoid fever, spending ten months in a hospital. Back in action, Holler was present at Appomattox Courthouse for Robert E. Lee's surrender in April 1865. Four years later, Holler came to Rock Hill where he opened a general store and built wagons, a trade that he had employed for the Confederacy.[3]

One of Holler's competitors was John Gary Anderson. After the deaths of his grandparents, Anderson had gone through a succession of legal guardians who, as he noted in his memoirs, were unsatisfactory. They paid little attention to him and mismanaged whatever modest inheritance he had received from his relatives. By 1881 Anderson was very much on his own. He had worked at the *Herald* newspaper, owned by James M. Ivy, but used his savings (and money owed him by one of his guardians) to purchase an interest in a grocery store. In his autobiography, he proclaimed, "For the first time in my life, I was in business! My! But I felt proud. I was one of the 'substantial business men' of the town." Promptly, he had the *Herald* print business stationery for him. Encountering Ivy, Anderson recalled the successful businessman saying, "Hello, Johnnie, what's this you are up to? I heard you have gone in business with my friend, Bill Roach, and I hope you'll succeed as I know you will."[4] There was about the young man an aura of confidence. When meeting "Johnnie," it was assumed that you were in the presence of one of Rock Hill's rising stars.

Anderson advertised his store with a prominent sign and notices in the *Herald*. He believed in telling customers about his produce, farm supplies and condiments. Reflecting on his use of promotion, Anderson wrote in 1937, "I was the pioneer in modern advertising in Rock Hill, not because of any special ability or foresight on my part, but because I had worked in newspaper offices and had had a better opportunity to see and 'feel' its effects." He also had developed a "feel" for a weak partnership, buying out Roach's interest, "of course on credit, for I had no money, and he accepted." Anderson then turned to his guardian, Iradell Jones, to come into the business, which was renamed (and re-signed) J.G. Anderson and Company. Steadily, the business expanded, largely on credit, into a restaurant, a farm implement store and dry goods establishment. Jones, like Roach, would be persuaded to give up his share in the company, and Anderson commented, "We parted friends." With both Roach and Jones, Anderson used credit obtained from local banks to consolidate his control of his business. In his early twenties, he had accomplished much from the time when he and his grandfather had arrived at the train depot in 1877.[5]

His marriage in 1884 to Captain Holler's daughter, Alice Louetta, further strengthened his standing in Rock Hill. Anderson, we would say, "married up," forming a marital union with someone of higher caste. As we have learned, Holler had already established himself in the town and the union of Anderson and Alice Louetta Holler produced children as well as a new company, Holler and Anderson Buggy Company. The concern was chartered in 1886 at the same time as the birth of the first Anderson child, Genevieve Louetta. Of course, carriages and Anderson went back together to the Civil War years when his grandfather Thomas built wagons for the Confederacy. Now, in the mid-1880s, carriages were increasingly popular. Holler and Anderson Buggy Company benefited from the public's need for modern transportation. Both Captain Holler and Johnnie Anderson had been in business in the city and had a good understanding of the market for the vehicles. Additionally, Holler, the carpenter, had constructed wagons for the South in the war.[6]

Anderson, the new husband and father, had interests other than the buggy business. In 1887 he purchased stock in the Standard Cotton Mill, one of the town's first textile mills. That same year, he strung a telephone line from the depot, where buggy components arrived, to the Holler and Anderson factory so he could check on shipments. The town was fascinated with this means of communication. Other businessmen would stop by the factory to use the crude telephone. By 1895 Anderson had joined with other subscribers to establish the Rock Hill Telephone Company. He added membership in a local real estate development partnership to his portfolio. In this venture, he often partnered with Cherry, the master at land speculation.[7]

It was the buggy business that took center stage in his life. Holler and Anderson Buggy Company had been chartered in 1886 with modest resources. It was capitalized with $8,000 three years later. By 1892, the company was incorporated with $25,000. In his memoirs, Anderson observed that in the 1880s and 1890s "there happened to be a few leaders of vision, courage and enterprise that are rarely found in small towns or villages; or, if found, hardly ever remain." He was among that elite. By the close of that era, he and Alice Louetta had six children: Genevieve Louetta, John Wesley, Mary Christine, Carrie, William Adlai and Alice Ellwood. And John Gary Anderson, the hungry orphan, had become one of those men of "vision, courage and enterprise."[8] His vision would reach into the realm of higher education as Rock Hill vigorously pursued Winthrop College, an

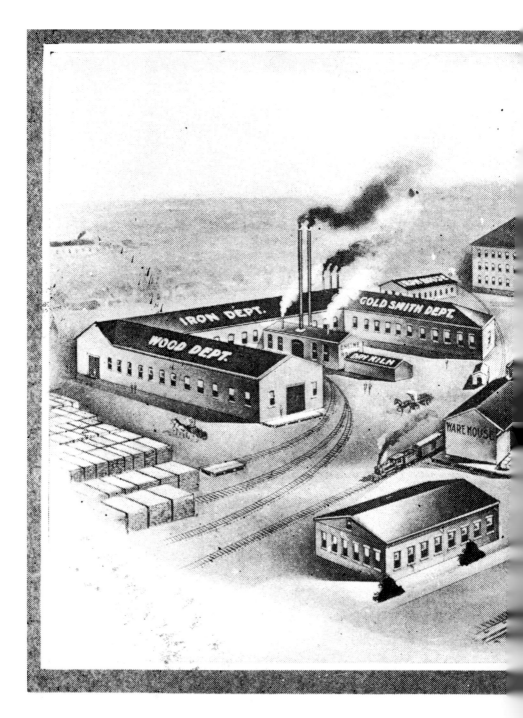

In the last days of the nineteenth century, the buggy factory bustled with activity. The company used the slogan "a little higher in price, but…"—the same advertising words adopted by Anderson for his automobile enterprise two decades later.

institution based in the capital city of Columbia. A college would strengthen Rock Hill; it was an enterprise that Anderson wanted for his town.

By 1890 Winthrop had outgrown its Columbia facilities, forcing the college's board of trustees to consider finding a new home for the school. In July of that year, Dr. Edward Joynes made a speech in Florence in which he advocated that the Winthrop Training School be offered to the state for support.

Governor Benjamin Ryan Tillman, champion of the state's farmers, was enthusiastic about the idea and, at Joynes's suggestion, appointed a committee that "endorsed the union of industrial and normal training and recommended that an act be passed providing for the foundation of a State Industrial and Normal College for Women."

On December 23, 1891, the state ratified the act establishing the South Carolina Industrial and Winthrop Normal College. On the same day, the legislature elected a board of trustees for the college and stipulated that the governor would serve as chairman of the board. The legislature also authorized the use of one hundred convicts to work as laborers for the construction of the college's buildings.

One of the first actions of the newly elected board of trustees was to open bids to South Carolina cities that wanted to serve as the college's location. Advertisements were placed in state newspapers for thirty days. When the board met in March 1892, the only cities to make offers were Anderson and Columbia. At first Anderson's bid seemed the more attractive of the two—an offer of $75,000 plus land to build on—but a court ruled the city's bonds invalid. After bids were reopened, Rock Hill and Spartanburg became the leading contenders. Captain Holler and John Gary Anderson had lobbied for their city's entry into the bidding war and mobilized the town's residents.

Since the board was having difficulty choosing between the two, its members decided to visit each city in order to make the proper decision. Unfortunately for Spartanburg, the board's visit coincided with the laying of the cornerstone of Converse College, an event that undoubtedly influenced its decision. That city now had its own college and did not need another school, John Anderson suggested.

Rock Hill's bid showed strong community support for the new college. In a referendum, an overwhelming 273 of 297 ballots favored a bond issue of $60,000. Eager to attract the college, Rock Hill also offered a choice of two sites on the outskirts of town. Interestingly, the selected site, Oakland Avenue, was the location of John Gary Anderson's home.

When the ten members of Winthrop's board of trustees met on April 2, 1893, their sentiments were clear—eight votes for Rock Hill and two for Spartanburg. Triumphant in its efforts to attract Winthrop

College, the town celebrated jubilantly. As bells rang and factory whistles blew, a band led more than a thousand townsfolk in a victory march through the city.

A delegate from Winthrop's board of trustees visited Rock Hill on June 1, 1893, to settle details about the bonds and the site for the college. Sixty bonds of $1,000 each were deposited in the Rock Hill First National Bank, and the Oakland Avenue site was chosen as the college's future home. Two Rock Hill businessmen, Dr. T.A. Crawford and W.J. Roddey, were then elected trustees.[9]

With the site chosen, the Winthrop board of trustees moved quickly to build the campus. The board selected the Atlanta firm of Burne and Morgan, which had designed the Clemson College campus in 1891, to design the first building.

On May 12, 1894, the birthday of Robert C. Winthrop, who had secured funds for the college that bore his name, festivities for the laying of the cornerstone of Winthrop's impressive new main building took place. Robert C. Winthrop, unable to attend because of poor health and advancing years, wished the new college well, saying, "May it continue to be, for centuries to come, an ornament and a support to the state which has so wisely and liberally funded it."[10]

At 9:00 a.m. marshals started to assemble in the streets. An estimated ten thousand spectators came from all corners of the state. Trains brought the entire Clemson College student body of five hundred to Rock Hill.

At noon, the official ceremony began in front of the main building. Ira D. Jones, speaker of the South Carolina House of Representatives, praised the educational progress of the state as mirrored in Winthrop's rapid development. Governor Tillman then observed the historic date, saying, "We have met to celebrate with fitting ceremonies the laying of the cornerstone of this state institution of learning."

At 1:00 p.m., a hushed silence fell as workmen lowered the cornerstone at the east front corner of the new building. As the stone nestled into place, a crescendo of cheers rose. For many of the dignitaries in attendance, including Anderson, years of hard work had finally come to fruition.

There was a feeling throughout the state that this was an important day in South Carolina history. The *State*, in an editorial typical of South Carolina newspapers, wrote: "This day marks the opening of an era of state aid in the education of women in South Carolina. It is an era of which all may be proud, and may join in the celebration of its inauguration. Heretofore, the state has devoted its money to the education of its men. But now…it says that women of South Carolina must no longer grow up in ignorance because they are poor."[11]

"Gardening, Winthrop College. Rock Hill,

Winthrop College, an institution that trained South Carolina's women, relocated from Columbia to Rock Hill in 1894. The college, led by President D.B. Johnson and Anderson's bold entrepreneurship, fueled the rapid growth of the New South city.

In the autumn of each year, cotton was harvested and transported to Rock Hill for sale. Anderson believed that the region had become too dependent on one crop.

John Gary Anderson had served as an enthusiastic promoter of Rock Hill as an attractive new home for Winthrop. After the college relocated to Rock Hill, Anderson joined the board of trustees, serving for nearly two decades. Frequently, President David B. Johnson walked down tree-lined Oakland Avenue to the stately Anderson home. He and Anderson would sit on the porch and discuss the progress taking root all about them in the New South city.[12]

By the time Winthrop arrived in Rock Hill in 1894, the New South city was booming. Entrepreneurs like Ivy, Cherry, Holler and Anderson worked in concert with President Johnson. The college made the city distinctive. Old South neighbors such as Chester and York lacked institutions of higher education. A women's college, admittedly a *white* women's college, fueled economic growth. An analysis of Rock Hill's population prior to and after Winthrop's relocation demonstrates the positive impact the school had on the community. As previously stated, only 100 people resided in Rock Hill in 1860; a decade later, the population was 270. As the railroad town grew as a center of commerce, the population numbered 2,744 citizens in 1890. Ten years later, 5,485 people called Rock Hill home. By 1912 the population was 12,000; in just a two-year period (1910–12), a dramatic total of 5,000 new residents flowed into town looking for opportunities.[13]

Textile mills, cotton farmers, educators and Anderson and Company partnered to build a rapidly growing community. Chief draftsman of this rosy economic blueprint was John Gary Anderson. It appears that he was everywhere, contributing to everything that would benefit the community. He, D.B. Johnson and the other town leaders guided the town with confidence and skill. Their confidence was contagious, and they wished to share it with everyone.

# More than a Social Club

*On certain occasions when Rock Hill has treated me like a red headed stepson,*
*I have felt like spanking it.*
*John Gary Anderson,* Autobiography

The success of Holler and Anderson pleased the Rock Hill boosters who advocated a diversified economy. The addition of a buggy manufacturing factory to the town's numerous ventures, such as textile mills and the relocated college, was considered crucial to the growth and vitality of Rock Hill. The *Yorkville Enquirer* noted that Holler and Anderson, along with another Rock Hill concern that manufactured buggies and furniture, were quite successful: "The entire output of the two establishments is consumed by the surrounding country. The quality of their productions is so far superior, as regards durability, etc., to the same class of goods manufactured at the North that neither factory is able to even supply the local demand."[1]

Of course, quality and durability of the goods was an important factor in Holler and Anderson's success. Their success was also attributed to the practice of "excellent business qualities." The comparison of their Southern-made goods to those of Northern origin was something that Anderson faced throughout his career.[2] He relished the comparison, believing his products to be superior.

Even with the positive response to the buggies produced by Holler and Anderson, the two men were unable to expand their operations because they lacked the capital. In 1891 Anderson approached his friend James M. Cherry and offered him shares in the company in return for financing. The two men were well acquainted. Both men had immigrated to York County, Cherry from Chester and Anderson from Lawsonville. Cherry's bank, the Savings

Bank of Rock Hill, was one of the first in Rock Hill. It grew out of a loan and trust company formed by a group of Rock Hill merchants in 1882. At first, Cherry was hesitant about the buggy factory. He believed that a Southern buggy factory could not possibly compete against the giant factories located in and around Cincinnati. Anderson changed Cherry's mind when he received a large contract from a merchant in Savannah. Promptly, Cherry invested in the business. At the time, Anderson believed that it was wise to bring someone into the company who had connections to the capital resources of the area. The new company was named the Rock Hill Buggy Company.[3]

Anderson was able to convince Cherry, along with his board of directors, to increase the capital of the company in order to build a larger factory on three acres of land adjacent to the Columbia-Charlotte Railroad. The Rock Hill Buggy Company purchased the Carolina Buggy Company—located in nearby Yorkville—soon after and used its machinery to equip the new factory. The Carolina Buggy Company was Anderson's only significant local competition and now it had been absorbed.[4]

The new factory provided Anderson the ability to manufacture up to 1,200 buggies per year. In 1892 it was estimated that the factory was large enough to handle the growing business for a number of years. Anderson was content with his new production facilities but not convinced that he knew enough about buggy manufacturing. Encouraged by the company's first traveling salesman, Richard H. Jones, Anderson went to Cincinnati in 1894 to learn more about the technological advances and mass production techniques of buggy manufacturing.[5]

While in Cincinnati, Anderson also began to formulate the way he would market his Rock Hill Buggies. Anderson realized that his operation in Rock Hill could not match the cost efficiency of the giant Cincinnati manufacturing firms. He knew that he had to devise a way to contend with the lower prices of his competition. He had to offer a better vehicle. The quality-versus-cost debate would arise later as Anderson battled cheaper, Northern-manufactured automobiles. Throughout his career, Anderson's credo remained "Nothing could be finer."

By the late nineteenth century, Cincinnati had become the center of the buggy manufacturing industry in the United States. Through this concentration, numerous innovations in production techniques emerged. The result was a dramatic reduction in the cost of production and in the retail price of Cincinnati buggies. But the trend toward greater production and lower prices also caused consumers to associate "Cincinnati work" with cheap and substandard work.

Anderson decided to stress the quality of Rock Hill Buggies as well as the expert workmanship used in their manufacture, adding an element of style that seemed to have been forgotten in the mass production of buggies. Anderson coined a marketing phrase, "a little higher in price, but…" in order to emphasize that the higher price of Rock Hill Buggies was related to quality.[6] Throughout his automotive career, Anderson stressed quality above all else. Unfortunately, he was slow to grasp the appeal of low prices such as those offered by Detroit's Henry Ford. To Anderson, nothing could be finer than his vehicles. Unfortunately, the consumer often opted for cheaper rather than finer.

Anderson was also determined to build a buggy that restored the style absent from the construction of Cincinnati buggies. He believed that the Cincinnati product lacked color, ornamentation, was too bulky and was "as plain as an old shoe." He later admitted that by adding a flair to his product he was specifically targeting the Southern market: "I determined to put style, and color, and life, into Rock Hill Buggies that would make its appeal to the esthetic Nature of the Southern people, and thus partly overcome the handicap which I was laboring."[7]

Anderson redesigned his line of buggies in 1894, the year Winthrop came to Rock Hill, to reflect his new marketing strategy:

> We at once redesigned…cutting down on sizes, changing lines here and there, reducing weight…The gear and wheels were painted a deep, rich red, and then striped and ornamented profusely in black and gold—the gold was the real thing, not an imitation…The body was finished in conventional black, but striped and ornamented to match the gear. The cushion of black moleskin. All mountings—seat rail, dash rail, seat handles, arm rails, hub bands, shaft tips, etc.,—were silver plated, instead of conventional black.[8]

The change in design and marketing strategy was a success. Orders for the flashy Rock Hill Buggies rolled into the factory, and beautiful buggies rolled out across the South.

The factory was running at full capacity. Anderson's payroll had increased from twelve employees to sixty-five in 1895. The Rock Hill Buggy Company accounted for about 10 percent of the city's manufacturing payroll. Yearly sales were estimated from $60,000 to $75,000. Anderson hired another traveling salesman and two covered the Southern states. The name Rock Hill Buggy was quickly becoming a familiar brand throughout the South.[9]

The growth of business for Anderson was not always achieved with such ease. He faced numerous problems in the Southern economy that made it difficult for many industries to survive. The depression that started in 1893 was particularly harmful to the predominantly agricultural South, and the periodic low cotton prices reduced his market even further. As long as Anderson's market remained the South, he was faced with the adverse effects of low cotton prices on his sales. Hard-pressed farmers were in no mood to purchase flashy buggies.

Anderson continued to experiment with different styles and color formats for his buggies, always looking for a competitive edge. He introduced a light rosewood color and an imitation oak body, as well as silver bronzed running gear, to the public in hopes of keeping their business. In 1896 Anderson created a body style that proved extremely popular.[10]

William Jennings Bryan was running for president on the Democratic ticket that year. One of the planks, the use of silver as a basis of the monetary system of the United States, was known as "16 to 1." The idea was extremely popular with Southern farmers who saw it as the answer to their economic woes. Inflating the value of silver would put more money in the pockets of the working class, especially farmers. Anderson capitalized on the support for Bryan's "16 to 1" plan among Southerners by designing and stylizing a buggy that represented the plan:

> The body was painted rosewood, with the slogan, '16 to 1' in large figures, entwined in a scroll, directly below the seat...The gear was painted silver—aluminum bronze—and the wheels, '16 to 1,' that is, the sixteen spokes were painted silver and the one hub, gold![11]

Anderson's efforts paid off. By the end of the 1893 recession, the Rock Hill Buggy Company had grown even larger. In 1897 the number of employees rose to ninety-six and the payroll was approximately $525 per week. In addition to the two traveling company salesmen, there were about three hundred authorized dealerships throughout the South.[12]

Along with the growing popularity and recognition of Rock Hill Buggies in the South, Anderson was growing in stature among Rock Hill's town fathers. After touring the Rock Hill Buggy factory, one visiting dignitary from Atlanta commented that

> cotton mills in the south are common. We may talk about our little ice factories and saw mills and turpentine distilleries, cotton oil mills and compresses, but when I stand in the midst of such an institution as the Rock Hill Buggy Co., right in the midst of free and unlimited coinage of silver of '16 to 1,' I am convinced it is not free silver we need, it is more J.G. Andersons in the south.

Anderson's success in manufacturing buggies was considered the work of a genius by many who had believed manufacturing that utilized semi-skilled and skilled labor was impossible in the South. He was lauded as a man whose business acumen was unusual in the agricultural area below the Mason-Dixon line. In a region whose growing textile industry was touted as the future of the South, the Rock Hill Buggy Company was considered the major industry of the town.[13]

Anderson was gaining recognition among his fellow Southern buggy manufacturers as well as throughout the remainder of the country. In 1900 he was chosen as one of the vice-presidents of the Carriage Builders National Association. Among his fellow members in the organization were Schuyler Colfax, former vice-president of the United States; W.C. Durant; and C.D. Firestone. Later the newly formed Southern Vehicle Association, at its first organized convention in Charleston, South Carolina, elected Anderson its first president.[14]

Anderson had gone from a transplanted small-town entrepreneur in the South searching for a trade or profession that would provide him with a future to a successful Southern businessman who was firmly established and recognized not only in his region but also throughout the United States. He had broken out of an environment in the Piedmont region that economic historians David L. Carlton and Peter A. Coclanis believed "confin[ed] the entrepreneurial impulse," and forced entrepreneurs into "limited and unimaginative channels."[15] He was far from "confined" and certainly not "unimaginative."

As Anderson's business expanded, he became more convinced that the town of Rock Hill and the region lagged far behind the more industrialized areas of the country. Anderson believed that in order for the Rock Hill Buggy Company to compete on an equal basis with the rest of the nation, its environment—Rock Hill and the South—must reflect an attitude of industry, modernity and progress. The relocation of Winthrop from Columbia was just part of his strategy. In order to grow, Rock Hill needed to attract both industry and workers. Anderson set out to improve the economic welfare of the region and to control an environment that was at times hostile to his efforts.

One of the vehicles on which Anderson relied to spread the word about Rock Hill and the South was the chamber of commerce. Chambers of commerce throughout the South in the early part of the twentieth century served as a way to organize the interests of the various businessmen, bankers and merchants. That interest was to promote the economic welfare of the town and its new leaders. Anderson, an emerging leader in Rock Hill, learned the benefits of advertising with his buggy business and believed Rock Hill needed an organization whose purpose was to promote the city.[16]

The various chambers also served as social clubs for the town's business class. Often, the chambers were criticized for being little more than informal recreational clubs. Rock Hill's chamber was no different. The Commercial Club of Rock Hill, founded in 1900, was the forerunner of the Rock Hill Chamber of Commerce. John Wood, the first full-time secretary of the Commercial Club, described the atmosphere of the organization when he first joined: "Interest had centered most largely in the comfortable reading rooms, billiard and pool tables and games of setback. Less popular…were the bathing facilities provided and the dining room which for a time was operated under independent management." An announcement in the *Herald* in 1903 told of improvements to the billiard room and attempts to expand the periodicals in the reading room.[17]

For two consecutive years, Anderson, who served as its president, explained in his annual presidential speech that the club was a "place of recreation and innocent amusement, where our businessmen and others can meet together." However, he was careful to note that the recreation was Christian in nature and that the club was a "moral institution… Drinking intoxicants, cursing and gambling are forbidden by rules…As an illustration of this fear of moral corruption within the Club, the 1903 Club banquet offered a speaker whose subject was 'The Social Club,' its Uses and Abuses."[18] Anderson had witnessed the adverse effects of alcohol on townspeople, and he was vigilant in his commitment to a sober, energetic New South community.

Regardless of these moral issues and concerns, the main purpose of the Commercial Club and later the chamber of commerce was to foster a "booster spirit" for economic independence and opportunity. The chief booster was John Gary Anderson. Such organizations also united merchants and other professional people into a distinct class, separate from the rural people and even other townspeople. The ability of Rock Hill's elite to attract industry, modernize the town and promote the growth of the community depended on their ability to present, at least outwardly, a consensus of action.

As president of the Commercial Club, Anderson's main accomplishment was to convince members that the organization needed a full-time executive to carry out the club's business. Until a professional administrator was in place, the club would remain little more than a men's club. Many civic organizations in Southern towns, especially ones that focused on civic improvements and economic development, hired someone to serve as a "professional booster." These boosters also provided management and supervision of the club's activities. In 1904 the Rock Hill club hired John Wood, a professional, as the club's first full-time secretary. Anderson developed the job description for the position. He outlined the duties of the secretary in his speech to the Commercial Club in 1904, stating that the secretary was responsible for opening the office, overseeing small road improvement projects and conducting general office work. The secretary was also in charge of soliciting industry to Rock Hill, as well as working to attract white, semi-skilled workers needed for the new factories in Rock Hill.[19]

Many of the projects that the Commercial Club developed were the same projects that Anderson championed. As president, Anderson pointed out that the club's mission was to build roads, establish factories and consider "any business proposition of a public nature that may be brought to its attention." Under Anderson's direction, the Commercial Club helped bring the U.S. Circuit Court of the Western Judicial district of South Carolina to Rock Hill and successfully lobbied for a new U.S. post office.[20] The club also supervised the maintenance of the major roads leading into the town.

In concert with John Wood, who criticized the club's inability to accomplish anything substantive for the community, Anderson realized that the Commercial Club was primarily a social organization. In his presidential address to the Commercial Club in 1904, Anderson sarcastically noted its lack of any real accomplishments. The organization still offered its members an environment of "good cheer and friendly feeling," which Anderson felt was crucial to the organization, but it failed to do anything of importance in the community. Feeling stymied by the club's inaction, Anderson was forced to look for another form of organized assistance.[21]

In reaction to his frustrations with the club, in 1906 Anderson pushed for the formation of another organization whose true focus was the betterment of the community, not the entertainment of its members. Relying on the Commercial Club's roster of members, Anderson helped develop the Rock Hill Chamber of Commerce. Chambers of commerce were appearing in towns and cities throughout the South during this period. All of the clubs were formed with the main objective of promoting business in their cities. The *Rock Hill Record* reported that the new chamber of commerce was "getting down to business for the good of the town." In the Rock Hill club's constitution and bylaws were the objectives Anderson personally advocated—promotion of manufactures, encouragement of diversified farming, attempts to secure fair railroad rates and the marketing of Rock Hill to potential industries. Through these efforts, the Rock Hill Chamber of Commerce's function was to promote the "general welfare of the community."[22]

Anderson was involved with the chamber until 1923, when, in his opinion, the focus of the organization changed. The chamber had significantly aided the "general welfare" of Rock Hill over the years by encouraging manufacturers, like Aragon Mills. It also supported Anderson's Rock Hill Plan (see next chapter), the Good Roads Movement, town and county electrification and various other community improvements.[23]

But when the Anderson Motor Company faced overwhelming financial difficulties in 1924, the chamber turned down a proposal from Anderson to back his company financially. Anderson perceived the chamber's refusal as its inability to realize the importance of his automobile factory. Had he not earned the town's support? Anderson believed that his payroll and the money that returned to Rock Hill from the sales of his automobiles was too important for the town's economic well-being for the chamber to ignore.[24] The Anderson Motor Company employed approximately one hundred workers, which was small compared to some of the area's cotton mills. Anderson felt that the duty of the chamber, as the representative of the business community, was to help keep important businesses like the Anderson Motor Company alive. The chamber disagreed. Although many of the community's banks and merchants supported—or were investors in—the local textile mills, those serving in the chamber of commerce refused to help Anderson save his automobile factory. Three years after Anderson had asked the chamber for help, the old Anderson Motor Company factory was leased to a bleachery. The chamber—his chamber—was involved in bringing the bleachery to Rock Hill when the Anderson factory was sold for taxes.[25]

# The Rock Hill Plan

*Let us demonstrate to the world that we mean business, not only this year*
*but for all years to come; that we have more business intelligence than to*
*work for them at a loss; that we are going to have a fair profit for our*
*cotton; that we are never going to be caught napping again.*
John Gary Anderson, The State, *November 9, 1911*

John Gary Anderson's vision reached beyond the "boosterism" of social clubs. Like his early partner J.M. Cherry, Anderson realized the link between agriculture and industry. Cherry would gain recognition as the Alfalfa King, an innovative farmer who marketed the grain and used his economic leverage to buy property and diversify. Anderson and Cherry grasped the tenuous situation faced by Southern farmers. Good years were overshadowed by bad years. Unfortunately, fluctuating cotton prices affected Anderson far more than they did Cherry, who would purchase land from the city limits to the Catawba River—land upon which Cherry Road would be constructed and economic growth could be sparked.[1]

Cotton's influence on the South's economy plagued Anderson throughout his career. He constantly worried that his business success was tied too closely to the South's cotton market; as the price of cotton went, so did the security of his company. Anderson was convinced if cotton's hold on the Southern economy could be minimized, then his business, along with others in the South, might stand a better chance of success. Cotton growers also understood the problems involved in the wildly fluctuating cotton prices. As long as the South depended on cotton, it remained at the mercy of a world market whose demand dictated the price. That demand often determined

A patriotic community, Rock Hill celebrated the nation's birthday on July 4, 1916.

the success or failure of many cotton growers, people who would—or would not—purchase buggies based on the price of cotton.

As a means to stabilize the South's cotton-based economy, Southerners attempted to control the price of cotton by limiting the output of the crop. Such efforts to control cotton prices began in the early nineteenth century. Dimos Ponce, a Georgia planter who worried about the low price of cotton, suggested a crop-control plan in 1844. Ponce was convinced that an informal pact among honorable planters to reduce cotton acreage would increase the price of cotton. Unfortunately, planters were unwilling to reduce their output, and the proposal failed.[2]

The post-bellum period brought further calls for the reduction of cotton production as a means of increasing its value. Farmers' alliances and cooperatives throughout the South called for cotton farmers to participate voluntarily in the reduction of the Southern cotton crop. Although the South Carolina State Farmers Alliance disbanded in 1892, farmers in the state were still able to organize and collectively call for a unified effort to reduce cotton output.[3]

Writing to the *Rock Hill Herald* in early 1893, a Lancaster County, South Carolina farmer called for area farmers to plant less cotton and grow more goods for personal consumption. He claimed that he had "never seen a farmer prosper by raising all cotton and buying all of his supplies for man and beast."[4] It was clear to the "old farmer" that the system of safety-first farming practiced in the South Carolina Upcountry in the early nineteenth century provided a more secure living. It protected the Southern farmer from the fluctuating cotton market, a market the farmer believed was controlled by Northern factories and worldwide demand. He called for farmers to grow cotton only as a surplus and use the proceeds from its sales for paying taxes.

Such calls went unheeded. More and more Southern farmers depended on cash crops, such as cotton, for their economic survival. If the price of cotton dropped, the farmers, if able, simply planted more cotton to make up the difference. In fact, cotton output in South Carolina increased throughout the early years of the 1890s depression—in 1893, 1894 and 1895.[5] The old farmer's call for growing less cotton signified a desire by some to stem the growing influence of modern capitalism on the South's rural economy. But others, such as Anderson, hoped the Southern farmer could control their cotton production as a means of competing in the New South's economy. He wished to see a regional approach to the problem.

Whenever the price of cotton fell below the break-even point, Southern farmers called for unity in solving the problem. Almost every time, reduction of the Southern cotton crop was touted as a solution to low cotton prices. When the price of cotton again fell below break-even in 1905, the Southern Cotton Association, a progressive coalition of Southern farmers, called for a concerted Southern effort to reduce production.[6] This time, unlike the increase in production in 1893–95, cotton acreage in the South decreased. There was no tangible evidence that the following year's reduction in cotton acreage was the result of their efforts. Cotton prices rose soon after the reduction because of a growing demand for cotton on the world market. Again, the movement to reduce cotton acreage dissolved soon after prices started to rise and the association disbanded in 1908. The crisis was over, it was reasoned.

Not only did the price of cotton affect the lives of Southern farmers, but it also determined the success of the Rock Hill Buggy Company. The 15,693,000 bales of cotton produced in 1911 set a record, but they also caused the price of cotton to plummet.[7] Anderson's buggy company faced potential financial ruin in 1911 when the price of cotton fell below five cents per pound, which was considered the break-even level. Much of his business was conducted on a credit basis. Many of the buggies advanced to authorized dealers were sold, but the buyers bought the buggies on credit. The dealers provided the credit to the buyers. Since the buyers were mostly rural farmers who relied on the profits from the sale of their cotton crop to pay their bills, they were unable to make payments on the loans. If they could not make the payments to the distributors, the distributors were unable to pay Anderson for the buggies. Thus, a ripple effect—or perhaps a tidal wave—made its way up the corporate ladder.

Anderson claimed that his buggy dealers owed him as much as $300,000. To receive any form of payment, Anderson was forced to accept cotton at eight cents a pound in lieu of cash for his buggies. He instructed the distributor to accept the cotton instead of a cash payment and warehouse the cotton until the prices rose. By late 1911, with the prediction of another record-breaking cotton crop and faced with the slowest part of the year for buggy sales, Anderson's business was in jeopardy. Continually plagued by the influence of cotton on his business, he responded by offering his own crop-reduction plan to the Southern cotton farmers. Called the Rock Hill Plan, the campaign received a tremendous amount of publicity and was one of the more recognized movements to control cotton prices. He openly admitted that above all the Rock Hill Plan was a self-serving act. But he also felt a degree of pride in helping his fellow Southerners.[8] If he survived, they would survive. All would benefit.

The Rock Hill Plan was simply a better-organized and well-publicized effort to reduce the cotton crop in the South. Like previous and future plans (such as FDR's New Deal), its goal was to restrict the output of cotton in order to spark an increase in its value. And like previous efforts, the plan received endorsements from farmers organizations such as the South Carolina Farmers Union, the National Farmer's Union and the Southern Cotton Congress. Anderson's plan proposed to "secure at comparatively insignificant cost borne by each county, the signature of each and every individual farmer to the pledge that he will reduce his cotton acreage for the year 1912 as compared with 1911, not less than 25 percent."[9]

What was interesting about Anderson's plan, as well as the efforts of the Southern Cotton Congress, was that they both emphasized diversified farming as a solution to the South's economic problems:

> *Cut down the cotton acreage and the South will not have to send west and north for foodstuff totaling an amount of actual money in figures which would stagger the imagination —millions upon millions every year, for meat, and grain, and hay, and mules, and shoes, and hats, and clothing and a thousand and one other things, which with the greatest ease and the greatest profit can be raised and produced on southern farms, and in southern factories.*[10]

Like the old farmer writing to the *Rock Hill Herald* in 1893, Southerners in the early twentieth century still feared total dependency on a modern

Anderson's economic interests reached far beyond manufacturing. He spoke frequently about the need for the region to diversify its economy. His Rock Hill Plan was designed to focus public attention on the pitfalls of King Cotton.

capitalistic economy. Anderson carried this theme of diversified economy throughout his business career. In a letter to John R. Shurley, president of the Rock Hill Chamber of Commerce, in 1922, Anderson explained the need for the city to diversify its industry. He also suggested that the outlying rural areas needed to diversify their crops. It was perilous to remain addicted to cotton with its fluctuating prices.

Anderson proposed that the city actively seek other sources of industry and agriculture. He realized that for the city to grow "we have got to bring more people here, and the only way to bring them here is to give them something to do. We ought to start something in the way of manufacturing enterprises."[11] He suggested creameries, poultry farming or tobacco growing—anything to alleviate the area's dependence on cotton.

Another interesting aspect of Anderson's plan was his recommendation for the development of county committees. He proposed that each committee consist of a merchant, a banker and a farmer. Since all three groups benefited from high cotton prices, Anderson believed that cooperation among these groups would be more effective. The county committees represented what Anderson saw as crucial to the success of the Rock Hill Plan: a coalition of business, capital and agriculture. It represented a new look for the South. According to Anderson, combining forces was the only way to win. John Gary Anderson believed in the old cliché that a rising tide lifts all boats.

Though Anderson knew that all three groups were affected by cotton prices, he faced a problem of finding a spokesman for the plan. He realized the plan needed a spokesman for the campaign who was acceptable to all—the farmers as well as the merchants and industrialists involved in the coalition. Aware that his own background in business made him unsuitable as the head of the movement, Anderson turned to E.J. Watson, the South Carolina state commissioner of the Department of Agriculture, Commerce and Industry. Watson also served as president of the Southern Cotton Congress, a group of Southerners organized to address the problem of cotton production. Since the Southern Cotton Congress already had an organization in place and Watson was its president, it was the perfect vehicle for the presentation of the Rock Hill Plan.

E.J. Watson was an excellent selection for the spokesman as well as a perfect match for Anderson. Like Anderson, Watson had campaigned to improve economic conditions in South Carolina. Much of his efforts paralleled Anderson's in helping South Carolina industrialize and modernize, while at the same time protecting the unique social system of South Carolina's ruling elite. Historian David Carlton noted that Watson's brand of reform reflected an attempt to stabilize a society whose social system was changing from a rural, agricultural one to a system based on both agricultural and industrial influences. Although South Carolina's reform programs appeared similar to those of the national Progressives, the goals were different.[12] Watson and Anderson both wanted a diversified economy, under the condition that the social classes stayed the same.

Watson displayed Progressive ideals in his efforts to regulate child labor in the mills, introduce modern roadways and attract industry and workers to the state. But, unlike the national Progressives who hoped to "institutionalize" reforms, Watson's efforts were meant to stabilize the social structure and preserve the New South's established political hierarchy. Watson was critical of Northern Progressives who traveled south to view the conditions of Southern mill workers. He called them "from-the-Pullman-car-window sociological tourists of the South."[13] Like Anderson, Watson advocated a hands-on approach to the region's problems.

Anderson also worked toward the same goals, first in Rock Hill and later throughout the South. Intent on creating a stable economic environment that would benefit his business, he also promoted many of the same measures as did Watson: roads, industry, government expenditures to promote economic stability and education, labor standards and health measures to ensure a viable workforce. The success of both programs meant personal success as well as the preservation of the state's ruling hierarchy.

With Watson's selection as a spokesman for the Rock Hill Plan, Anderson was ready to present the plan to the people of the South. He and Watson used the annual meeting of the Southern Cotton Congress in New Orleans as a kickoff for the start of the publicity campaign. The congress in December 1911 heartily adopted the Rock Hill Plan with only minor adjustments. Anderson, along with E.J. Watson and Charles S. Barrett, president of the National Farmers Union, began their state-to-state publicity campaign in January 1912.

Acceptance of the Rock Hill Plan throughout the South was enthusiastic. Anderson and Watson spoke to numerous state legislatures, merchant conventions and farmer's organizations. They spoke in Raleigh, Atlanta, Jackson, Montgomery, New Orleans, Baton Rouge, Memphis, Oklahoma City and other towns on their tour. They consulted state leaders in their efforts to introduce the plan to the farmer. Their tour received a great deal of coverage from local newspapers and appeared to be a complete success. The only cotton state they did not visit was Texas. Governor Colquitt of Texas informed Anderson and Watson that his state already had a cotton reduction plan in place and did not require a visit from them.[14]

In South Carolina, the House of Representatives endorsed the Rock Hill Plan. County committees were formed that reflected Anderson's desire to appoint merchants and bankers as well as farmers. The county committee of York County, where Rock Hill is located, appointed two merchants and bankers, Ira B. Dunlap and T.L. Johnston. The receipt and disbursement statement of the York County Committee listed numerous contributors to the Rock Hill Plan—banks, industry, cotton mills and even suppliers from New York. The plan was readily accepted by all who stood to profit from its success.[15]

Many farmers throughout the South voluntarily signed the pledge to reduce their cotton acreage by 25 percent. Numbers of merchants, bankers and politicians contributed token amounts to the campaign. According to the figures of cotton output from 1911 to 1912, it appeared that their efforts were successful. Cotton production throughout the South showed an overall reduction of about 13 percent and cotton acreage was reduced by about 16 percent.[16]

Farmers probably would have reduced their cotton acreage in 1912 regardless of the Rock Hill Plan. Most cotton growers who reduced their output did so not out of loyalty to the Rock Hill Plan, but because they were financially unable to plant as much cotton as before. With the price of cotton so low by the end of 1911, it was not wise to gamble on it rising

By 1910 many Southern farmers, unable to eke out a living on the land, came to cities like Rock Hill. This postcard features Carhartt Cotton Mill.

above the break-even level of 1912. Also, many farmers were heavily in debt and lacked the money or credit to plant full cotton crops in 1912. The reduction of the crop was probably a natural reaction by individuals to market forces rather than one caused by concerted political action. The Rock Hill Plan helped draw attention to the problems faced by all Southerners as long as cotton ruled the Southern economy. Its success lay in the bringing together of merchants, industry, capital and agriculture to combat an economic problem affecting all of the South. In concert, the region's constituencies could address the issue of overproduction of cotton.

Anderson applauded the results for which he had so energetically campaigned. Within a few months, the price of cotton had moved above the critical five-cent break-even mark. The cotton he had accepted at eight cents a pound in late 1911 as payment for his buggies rose to ten cents by April 1912. Anderson sold all the cotton he had warehoused the year before. He claimed amazingly to have lost only fifty-two dollars. Again, with the problem gone, farmers forgot the lesson, replanted cotton acreage and by 1914 faced a catastrophe they had not envisioned.[17]

War broke out in Europe in 1914 and its effects were felt worldwide. The effect on the Southern cotton crop was immediate. The English cotton market, as well as other European markets, were closed off from the South, and remained closed until the end of World War I. The prosperity experienced in the South after the 1911 "cotton crisis" soon disappeared as cotton exchanges shut down and remained closed for months. Cotton sold for rockbottom prices or not at all. Historian George B. Tindall described the reaction in the South as a "reverberation [that] shattered a midsummer's dream of comfort and security." Anderson described to one of his New York creditors the effect the war had on the South as having "knocked all our hopes up again, hitting the South harder than any other section."[18] The roller coaster had plunged again, despite the hard work of Anderson and his allies.

The Southern Cotton Congress, which had disbanded soon after the 1911–12 cotton crisis, was revived as a defensive measure against falling cotton prices. At its meeting in August 1914, the reestablished congress called for such extreme measures as state-level governmental control of cotton production. Anderson was confident that the congress could prevent the same kind of panic that arose in 1911. But neither plans for controlling the crop nor calls for fixed prices could counter the effects of the Great War.[19]

The federal government also offered to help the beleaguered South. In an effort to provide federal assistance to the cash-short cotton growers, Secretary of the Treasury William G. McAdoo allowed the use of cotton warehouse receipts as the basis for issuance of currency from the Federal Reserve (at 75 percent of their face value). David F. Houston, secretary of agriculture, claimed the acceptance of warehouse receipts by the Federal Reserve was the only thing that the federal government could do "under the Aldrich-Vreeland Law and the Federal Reserve Law."[20] The move provided cotton growers and the Southern economy an influx of cash, but with the value of cotton below the break-even point, it was not enough to cover current debts and avoid further losses on cotton production.

The situation grew worse as the price of cotton tumbled. The Southern Cotton Congress, in an extreme move, called for a complete withdrawal of the entire Southern cotton crop from the 1915 market. They favored warehousing the cotton crop and providing a small loan to cotton farmers until cotton prices rose high enough to earn the farmers a profit. The South once again geared up for a campaign to promote higher cotton prices. This time, Northerners were either recruited or joined in the campaign to help the South solve its economic crisis.[21]

This time, the most popular idea to control cotton prices revolved around the idea of creating a temporary market for the South's cotton crop. Individuals, businesses, corporations and government agencies were asked to buy a bale of cotton as a means of showing support for the South. The cause was called the buy-a-bale movement, and it attracted the attention of people in both Northern and Southern states.

Rock Hill hitched its economic wagon to two rising stars: Winthrop College and John Gary Anderson. This scene is of a well-stocked downtown store, circa 1915.

In the North, merchant associations in New York City heartily endorsed and supported the movement. President Woodrow Wilson, a native Southerner, bought "several bales…as a contribution to the 'buy-a-bale of cotton' movement in the South." F.L. Klingensmith, secretary of the Ford Motor Company, reiterated Ford's commitment to have its "branch houses in the South to follow the general plan in each 'buying a bale of cotton.' Even New York City hotels entered the craze to help the economically depressed South out of its predicament by buying a bale. One hotel, the McAlpin, placed a bale in the center of its lobby with a sign that "announce[d] that cotton is 'as good as gold.'"[22]

In the South, support for the buy-a-bale movement was equally enthusiastic and widespread. James Buchanan Duke's American Tobacco Company offered to buy "middling cotton" at ten cents per pound, provided the same amount of its tobacco product was purchased by the cotton seller. The Texas State Legislature passed a resolution calling for the exemption from state taxes of all buy-a-bale cotton purchased at ten cents per pound. Richard I. Manning, governor of South Carolina (and later board member of Anderson's company), "pleaded for the North and the big cities to 'stand by the South now' and secured the promise of the Baltimore [Merchants and Manufacturers] association to buy 20,000 bales." Even Southern women suffragettes pitched in to aid the movement.[23]

Not all reaction to the buy-a-bale movement was favorable. A New York dry goods business owner complained that the movement only temporarily stemmed the low prices of cotton. He argued that the buy-a-bale cotton purchased by individuals being held in warehouses would sooner or later flood the market, and cotton prices would again fall. Another merchant expressed his concern that price increases in cotton would be passed on to the manufacturers. And yet another New Yorker attacked the program as a scheme to promote an artificial demand. He believed it was better to let the price of cotton drop, so the following year's cotton acreage would decrease naturally.[24]

Anderson believed the efforts behind the buy-a-bale movement had a central theme: the South was in miserable shape financially, and like the needy, the South required assistance from those who were more prosperous. It infuriated him to see his region belittled by New York dilettantes who were attracted to the movement because of its uniqueness. At the McAlpin Hotel in 1914, the reigning society hostess used mini-bales of cotton as the price of admission to that fall's season of afternoon tea dances.[25]

When Anderson traveled to New York in January 1915, he stayed at the Hotel Martinque, a favorite hotel for many Southern visitors. As he entered the lobby, he saw a bale of cotton in the center of the room with a sign that read, "We have bought our bale to help the South, have you bought yours?"[26] Anderson, aggravated by what he saw as a dig against the South, lost his temper. A reporter for the *New York Times* witnessed the outburst and approached Anderson for an interview, which appeared in the following day's edition.

In the interview, Anderson expressed concern that the buy-a-bale movement was more injurious to the South than it was helpful. He stated that the "greatest obstacle to progress was not the physical condition in the South, but the 'unfounded obsession that the South was broke…the moral effect was bad…They created the idea of a bankrupt, impoverished land in which people were dying by the score. That was pure nonsense."[27] He also proposed that the South would right itself by moving away from a dominant cotton crop to one of diversified staples, such as wheat and corn.

One week later, Norman H. Johnson, secretary of the Southern Wholesale Dry Goods Association, was quoted along lines similar to Anderson. He believed that Southern cotton growers and merchants had taken advantage of the situation. The movement "exerted a bad influence on retailers and others in the South. These people…took advantage of the agitation over the alleged poverty prevailing in the South to postpone the payment of their accounts." Whatever the circumstances, the cotton farmer and the South survived the 1914 cotton crisis. Anderson hinted at yet another wide-scale crop-reduction scheme but little was done to promote it on the same scale as the Rock Hill Plan.[28]

The notion of a cotton crop–reduction plan persisted among Southern cotton growers. The idea returned with the recession of 1920. The South Carolina Cotton Association passed a measure calling for a 50 percent crop-reduction plan for 1921. The York County Cotton Association held a special meeting in Rock Hill and approved the state committee's resolution. This time, John Gary Anderson's name was absent from the list of supporters. Anderson had finally realized that the crop-reduction schemes were doomed to fail because they only lasted as long as the price of cotton was low. Anderson also faced the fact that the South was far from removing the problem of a cotton-dominated economy.[29]

Anderson, like J.M. Cherry, believed that diversification of agriculture and industry was part of the answer to cure the economic woes of the South. Anderson called for farmers to plant more than just cotton as a cash crop. He argued that tobacco, peaches and corn crops could be expanded throughout the South as alternatives to cotton. He even suggested that farmers in the Rock Hill area try to start growing grapes for raisins.

The success of Southern cotton mills proved that that industry was a viable addition to the region's economy. What concerned Anderson was that the cotton mills remained linked to the South's cotton crop. For industry to take hold in the South, and to prosper without unnecessary encumbrances, it needed its own independent identity. As long as textile manufacturing remained the only major industry in the Carolinas, the efforts of Anderson and other industrialists to introduce new industries was not taken too seriously. Also, industry linked to the cotton crop was unlikely to counterbalance the influence cotton had on the economy.

Unfortunately, Anderson reacted to good economic times in the same way the cotton growers did. As long as profits were earned from growing cotton, cotton farmers were content and concentrated their efforts on growing cotton, not controlling prices. By 1913, with the sales and profit of the Rock Hill Buggy Company rising steadily along with the rise in cotton prices, Anderson turned his attention to managing his factory. Anderson was content with the Rock Hill Buggy Company's sales figures. And until 1915, he was convinced that his business was once again safe from outside influences.

In the shadows of Winthrop's campus, the York County Fair was held each fall. The area's citizens turned out in huge numbers to parade their prize livestock and sample winning recipes.

# "A Little Higher in Price, But..."

*Customers can have it painted any color they want so long as it's black.*
*Henry Ford,* Time, *March 17, 1941*

The first two decades of the twentieth century were the Progressive era. The assassination of President William McKinley at the Buffalo, New York Pan-American Exposition in September 1901 marked the end of the Gilded Age. Since the removal of Federal troops from the South in 1877, the nation had focused its attention on industrial development. The plight of African Americans was ignored as Andrew Carnegie's steel mills, John D. Rockefeller's oil derricks and J. Pierpont Morgan's financial expertise dominated America's economy.[1]

These three bold entrepreneurs (or perhaps robber barons) and their allies were powerful men. They controlled the political arena, overshadowing presidents like Benjamin Harrison, Grover Cleveland and McKinley. The United States Senate was a millionaires' club, its members drawn from the friends of big business. America's social conscience was in hibernation. New immigrants from Eastern and Southeastern Europe flowed across the Atlantic Ocean to New York's Ellis Island, destined for the meatpacking plants of Chicago or the oil fields of Illinois or the steel mills of Pittsburgh.[2]

The death of McKinley, however, sparked a change in America's political, social and economic landscape. Theodore Roosevelt, the hero of San Juan Hill, galloped into Washington with energy and a Square Deal for the American people. He promised that there would be no "crookedness in

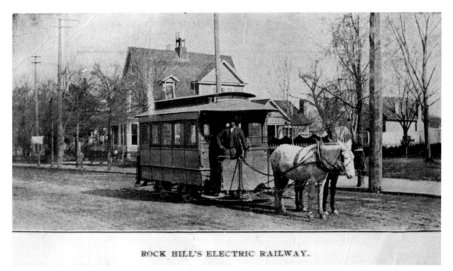

ROCK HILL'S ELECTRIC RAILWAY.

Near the Anderson Home on Rock Hill's Oakland Avenue, two mules, Elec and Tric, propelled a streetcar down the street, circa 1915.

the dealing." The playing field, for the first time in decades, would be level as he declared war on "bigness."[3]

Roosevelt's two successors, William Howard Taft and Woodrow Wilson, were also Progressives. Taft, an attorney, precisely attacked the trusts and monopolies such as Rockefeller's Standard Oil, which during the Gilded Age had held power in its hands. Wilson, a scholar and neophyte politician, also saw economic competition as part of his New Freedom program.[4]

The altered climate was ideal for men like John Gary Anderson. Even in conservative South Carolina, there were winds of change blowing. The dominant political figure, Benjamin Ryan Tillman, had endorsed the goals of the 1895 Cotton States Exposition in Atlanta. This fair, a tribute to the New South, highlighted the resurrection of the Southern economy. Tillman and a train full of state leaders journeyed to the capital of the New South and witnessed firsthand the power of industry. Textile mills were on the rise across the region. Farmers left depleted cotton fields and helped build textile empires like Springs Mills.[5]

In step with the philosophy of the New South, Colonel Leroy Springs built cities as well as mills. His investment in towns such as Lancaster, Fort Mill and Chester gave ex-farmers new jobs and helped fuel economic growth in the upstate of South Carolina. The same can be said of James Buchanan Duke, who, after cornering the tobacco market with his mass-produced cigarettes, invested in producing electricity for towns like Charlotte, Great Falls and Rock Hill. Duke Power would eventually become a regional force for channeling the water of the Catawba River into the waiting arms of industrialists. Electricity did more than light up the darkness; it brought employment to the South's people who had been through so much after the Civil War.[6]

John Gary Anderson was, as we have seen, shaped by the war and its aftermath. He had sought his future in the New South city of Rock Hill. By the Progressive era, Anderson was prepared to make the transition from buggy production to automobile manufacturing, although the change would not be smooth. Nevertheless, the country, especially the South, was willing to let an entrepreneur who treated his workers fairly experiment until he mastered the formula. And Anderson was in step with other Southern entrepreneurs—men like Springs and Duke.

As we have seen, John Gary Anderson was excelling in the early years of the twentieth century. His buggy company was producing 6,000 vehicles annually in 1900. Employees numbered between 100 and 125 men, and the pay reached $3 per day. The company—which Anderson liked to boast started with a $10 investment—was now valued at more than $250,000. He was recognized nationally for his leadership in the buggy industry. He was one of fifteen vice-presidents of the Carriage Builder's Association, which pointed out in an annual report that, although five years earlier auto enthusiasts had said the horse would soon become a curiosity, only 125 autos had since appeared in New York City. In fact, one commentator scoffed at the idea that the motor would ever replace the farm horse: "I know a little something of the prudence of the farmer, and I am not disposed to believe that he will ever pay from three to four hundred dollars for an electric motor; neither do I believe he will ever be persuaded to place a hydro carbon or other motor that depends ever so little upon a flame under a load of hay or grain." This report concluded that the carriage had nothing to fear from the auto since the latter would never provide a cheap means of transportation.[7]

Nevertheless, like Studebaker and others, Anderson realized that the buggy's days were numbered. As early as 1910, his sons, especially John Wesley Anderson, were experimenting with gasoline engines and thinking about the transition to autos. In March of that year, a bold headline in the *Record* proclaimed, "John G. Anderson Will Manufacture Automobiles." The first model was already being assembled. It would be a "high-grade" item with a thirty-horsepower, four-cylinder engine. Seating four persons and costing $2,500, it would offer a simple mechanism, fine materials and superb workmanship. A few days later the *Charlotte Observer* had praise for the neat, ivory-colored car Anderson displayed in that city. Without top, it would sell for $2,250. According to the *Observer*, Anderson was already seeking North Carolina sales agents.[8]

Apparently, neither agents nor customers overwhelmed him. Perhaps this pioneer model failed to function properly, or maybe it was a matter of price. At that time one could buy a Ford in Rock Hill for only $1,000. In addition, the buggy factory was in the midst of a banner year and in December 1910 added night shifts to meet anticipated demand. There seemed no reason to abandon buggies; but three years later, in June 1913, Anderson was once more thinking about autos. The 1912 season was disappointing; Anderson told a Charlotte reporter that business was off one-third and had been poor since the fall of 1911. In fact, because of these conditions, he originated and pushed his Rock Hill Plan, hoping to aid farmers who owed him money. As we have seen, this plan attracted wide attention and won the endorsement of many Southern leaders. Even if acreage was not actually cut, confidence in cotton was restored and prices rose somewhat. In this interview, Anderson said the era of the horse and buggy was past.[9]

And he marched into the New Frontier two years later. The buggy company published a twelve-page catalogue of "Anderson-made" bodies designed to fit a Ford chassis. Early in 1916 John Gary Anderson finally announced specific plans to begin assembling his own auto—body, chassis, the whole works. In his *Autobiography*, he recalled building only six experimental cars in 1916, but apparently he was referring to hesitant steps taken between 1910 and 1915, since operations were well under way by 1916. During January of that year, the Rock Hill Buggy Company held a spectacular "open house" for prospective dealers and local residents, many of whom, it was hoped, would become customers or stockholders of both. Instead of buggies, they saw several Anderson Cars bathed in electric lights, listened to soft music and enjoyed light refreshments. The whole affair, said the *Record*, was like a "family gathering." And the newspaper commented that many compliments were showered upon "Quiet John." The high point of the week was a banquet at the Carolina Hotel. Among the speakers were Anderson's friend, Dr. D.B. Johnson, president of Winthrop College; Joseph A. Anglada, Anderson's chief engineer and designer; and John C. Kilgo, a Methodist bishop from Charlotte.[10]

During these same weeks, the first car was delivered to T.L. Johnston, president of the People's National Bank of Rock Hill. On February 7, the *Record* pointed with pride to the first out-of-town customer, the owner of the *Anderson (SC) Intelligence*. National trade publications soon took note of what was happening in South Carolina. *Horseless Age* announced the new Anderson Six, and *Automobile Topics* (March 25, 1916) said that after two years of quiet preparation, the "Anderson 6-40-6" had made its appearance for $1,250 (Free On Board, or FOB, Rock Hill). It had a Continental forty-horsepower, six-cylinder engine capable of delivering thirty-eight

COPYRIGHTED BY R.M.LONDON, ROCK HILL, S.C. 1907.

WINTHROP COLLEE, ROCK HI

actual horsepower at 200 revolutions per minute, Westinghouse electrical equipment (including a trouble lamp complete with cord and cigar lighter), twelve-spoke wheels made of the best South Carolina hickory and thirty-three-by-four-inch oversized tires. Special equipment made the Anderson Car unusually attractive. These extras included a one-man top with quickly detachable side curtains and an envelope in which to put them, running board with luggage straps, power-driven tire pump with gauge and tubing, ventilating windshield, sixty-mile-per-hour speedometer and a complete set of tools and wrenches.

The two standard bodies (six-passenger touring car and three-passenger roadster) were painted Brewster green with black fenders and hood. At additional cost, a customer could get other color combinations, a heating system and rumble seats for the roadster. *Automobile Topics* told readers the Anderson offered a freight saving of some fifty dollars and a homemade product that should appeal to Southern customers. A few weeks later the *Automobile* (April 20, 1916) hailed the "Anderson Six" as "a new car manufactured in a new territory…a good unit assembled in a neat chassis with extra lavish equipment."[11] Rock Hill was the capital city of this "new territory," and John Gary Anderson and his advisors sensed a golden opportunity to serve the New South.

There are no reliable production figures for these early years but Anderson was evidently pleased with the demand. On December 1, 1916, he applied to the South Carolina secretary of state for a charter. His letterhead, already confidently displaying the words "Anderson Motor Company," reserved the largest letters for the Rock Hill Buggy Company and carried that concern's

This panoramic view of Winthrop's expanding campus (1907) shows the development of the college, where Anderson served as trustee until his death in 1937.

famous trademark—two rams butting their heads together—and the slogan "A little higher in price, but…" During the early 1920s, the Anderson Car would adapt this slogan to its own special needs: "A little higher in price, but made in Dixie!" Originally, according to the *Record*, Anderson proposed as a sales slogan, "The car that sells itself."[12]

According to this petition, the motor company would be capitalized at $1.5 million. There would be 150,000 shares with par value of $10 per share. One half of this issue would be common stock; the other half percent preferred. The petitioners proposed to manufacture, assemble, buy, sell and generally deal in automobiles, motor trucks and other vehicles, as well as supplies and accessories. They were also to carry on any trade or business incidental thereto or connected with the enterprise.[13] In return for the buggy company and its assets, Anderson received all common stock and $250,000 in preferred stock. The remaining 50,000 shares were offered to the public at $10 each, payable 20 percent cash, 20 percent in ninety days, 10 percent quarterly thereafter. An ad appearing soon after incorporation announced the company had orders for all the cars it could produce in 1917. This meant over $1 million in sales and a payroll of $100,000. The ad enthusiastically noted,

> *We predict that this enterprise is to be a great money maker. Some of the Detroit factories, making a car at over $1,000.00 have paid dividends this year of nearly 200 per cent. These factories are turning out five thousand cars per annum. Why can't this be done in the South—even in Rock Hill? It can and we believe it will. You have an opportunity of getting in on the*

# VISITORS WELCOME

## FOR INFORMATION WRITE

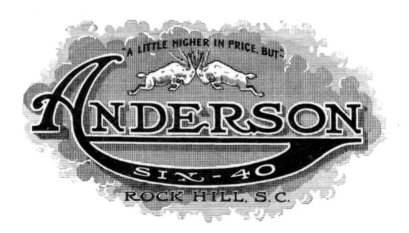

# ANDERSON MOTOR CO.

Anderson believed in the power of advertising. By 1916 he had transformed his buggy company into one that manufactured sleek automobiles.

*"ground floor." Will you do it, or will you hold back and let the "other fellow" get in and then in a year or two moan your ill luck? You can't possibly lose anything—because the business is going to be conservatively and efficiently managed—but you have the chance of making a SMALL FORTUNE. Will you take it?*

*Men of wide experience—in the $100,000 class—will associate themselves with us in the active management of the business. The only way you can really lose anything on this proposition is to hold your pocketbook with a death grip and let the "other fellow" take the chance. You have a fine opportunity to build yourself and your town.*

*It's up to you.*

Among the captains of industry watching Anderson was James B. Duke, the tobacco and power magnate. He offered Anderson $1 million to move the company to Charlotte, site of the stately Duke Mansion. Anderson graciously declined; Rock Hill was his home.[14] The entrepreneur envisioned his city as the spoke in the automobile wheel. From Rock Hill, Anderson would spin a corporate empire stretching across the Southland.

Early in 1917, these company officers were elected: J.G. Anderson, president; J.W. Anderson, vice-president; and C.J. Henry, secretary-treasurer. In addition to the Andersons (father and son), the board of directors included T.L. Johnston, a local banker; Alex Long, a Rock Hill textile executive; Cliff Williams, president of a Mississippi machine company; St. Elmo Massengale, an Atlanta advertising man; and W.H. Barber, president of Citizens' Bank of Moultrie, Georgia. Those officers were an impressive team and they appeared, at first glance, to give Anderson a solid capital base.

Theoretically, of course, if 50,000 shares were sold to the public at $1,000 each, early in 1917 the Anderson Motor Company had half a million in working capital less the cost of the sale. But stock didn't move that well, for on February 12, 1917, the company offered one share of common stock free with every two shares of preferred. Anderson said he would soon be producing 2,500 to 5,000 cars a year, and this would mean a profit of 30 to 75 percent on common stock. "This is not a wild statement," he added. "It can and will be substantiated on request."[15] Ever the confident promoter, Anderson believed that his venture would soon attract investors and customers.

Three days later, another ad pointed out that the company was completely free of debt. It expected to produce 1,200 cars in 1917, 3,000 in 1918 and not less than 5,000 to 6,000 by 1920. Actually, this matter of numbers is intriguing. On page 516 of his *Autobiography* Anderson stated his original goal was only 600 units a year, an output that would equal the profits of the buggy company. But on page 522 it seems that even at the outset he had 2,500 cars in mind—a considerable difference!

In 1917, buoyed by the success of early production efforts, the Anderson Motor Company printed a lavish brochure stressing the many years of buggy-building experience behind each auto and detailing the great care with which an Anderson was made.

> *You will find all Anderson bodies distinctly original and exclusive in design. You will find the upholstery deep and wide, stuffed with real curled hair and carefully tailored in real leather. You will find the finish of lasting luster, hand applied and hand rubbed, involving twenty-one distinct operations in all. All Anderson cars are built on the same chassis and all cars have the same equipment. Only the body designs are different.*[16]

In addition, this booklet stressed the 120-inch wheelbase, 2,750-pound weight and perfect balance. "It is powerful. It will travel from two to sixty miles per hour on [six] high." An Anderson Car, the reader was assured, was simple to control, economical to operate. It had a big mahogany steering wheel, large clutch and brake pedals and plenty of "pep and power." One owner (Allan Gibson of Swainsboro, Georgia) attested to the fact that the Anderson was a sturdy car:

> *I bought one of your six-passenger cars from Dixie garage of this place about three months ago and have driven it 8,000 miles with a perfect score, until I accidentally ran off a bridge some eighteen feet high into water where some drift logs had lodged. The car turned a complete somersault, landing bottom upwards with only damage to fender and windshield. I got the car out by the use of a stump puller and started it up without the least trouble and it is running as good today as it did the day I bought it.*
>
> *I have owned six cars, some of them high priced cars, and consider the Anderson superior to any of them. It is a good car for all purposes and well worth the money.*

When this brochure was originally printed, the price of an Anderson was $1,295, but a special note cautioned customers that as of July 15, 1917, each car would cost an additional $100. Undoubtedly, the Rock Hill firm was feeling the pinch of wartime shortages. And, although the United States government did not actually limit auto production until August 1918, Anderson was already looking toward Washington for war contracts. With the aid of Senator Benjamin Ryan Tillman, whom Anderson had

from selected hardwood stock... screwed together and glued in a fully accurate manner.

Anderson bodies are unique in that they are an Anderson product from the time the timber leaves the native forest till the final stages of finished body. Thousands of acres of hardwood timber land in the mountains of Western South Carolina, owned by the Anderson Company, insure an ample supply for years.

Dealers visiting the Chicago Show are invited to inspect our exhibit at the Coliseum as well as at the showrooms of Nicholson-Huff Company, 2111 Michigan Avenue.

**ANDERSON MOTOR COMPANY**
*Rock Hill*         *South Carolina*

Anderson advertised nationally. This ad appeared in the January 24, 1920 issue of the *Saturday Evening Post*.

known since they had worked together on relocating Winthrop College from Columbia to Rock Hill, he was able to secure some contracts, but just how many is not clear. Commenting that he had several contracts in hand, Anderson advertised in the *Record* for carpenters, painters, woodworkers and laborers "to help beat the Germans." In his *Autobiography*, Anderson speaks of orders for some three thousand small trucks. The *Rock Hill Record* mentions a contract for two hundred trucks, hinting that perhaps a thousand more would be built in the future. Anderson says the war ended so abruptly that only a "hundred or so" were finished and shipped. However, the company did build aviation trailers valued at nearly $500,000. These four-wheeled vehicles carried airplanes behind the trucks. Despite hectic times, the youthful motor company managed to serve the patriotic needs of the nation, gain valuable experience and at the same time turn a healthy profit. Interestingly, Anderson's descendants believe that numerous cars or trailers made their way to Europe during the conflict.[17]

Encouraged by this new vigor, the directors voted in September 1918 to increase capital stock to $2,625,000. Significantly, while "butting" rams remained, the buggy company had disappeared from Anderson's stationery. Cars—not buggies—were now his focus. There were only the words "Anderson Motor Company." Writing to the secretary of state

Winthrop and the Anderson family were Oakland Avenue neighbors. This postcard, circa 1920, features the imposing tower of Main Building (now called Tillman Hall).

Anderson's cars were painstakingly manufactured. This photograph illustrates the orderly production line, circa 1920.

on October 2, 1918, and enclosing a check to cover stock increase fees, Anderson dutifully signed, "Yours for the Fourth Liberty Loan." In June 1919, capital stock was increased another million to $3,625,000, the highest point in the company's brief history.[18]

These moves reflect, of course, the keen optimism of the automotive world in general. Throughout 1919, motor stocks rose phenomenally. Manufacturers could not build fast enough to meet the postwar demand. They had to contend with labor unrest, shortages of fuel and basic materials and faulty rail service; but from the armistice in 1918 until April 1920, dealers could sell at almost any price. Since banks viewed auto loans with considerable distrust, finance companies did a booming business. While consumers fell head over heels in love with the automobile, bankers were influenced less by their hearts and more by their wallets. An executive of the North Carolina National Bank based in Charlotte, North Carolina, told this tale of early auto financing: About 1910 a customer entered a local bank and told the president he had bought a car and needed a loan. The president obligingly wrote out two copies of the agreement. The customer signed, and then the president asked for the keys to the car. These, along with the bank's copy of the agreement, he dropped into a desk drawer. Then, turning to the startled customer, he said, "Now, pay back your loan and you get your keys."

In November 1919, Anderson advertised for more workers, pointing out that production must soon reach 500 cars per month. There was a wild scramble for Anderson stock in South Carolina, especially in the Rock Hill area. During January and February of 1920 the *State* printed numerous ads from those people seeking to buy stock. A Greer resident offered to pay 8 percent interest and assume any balance due the company. Apparently well-to-do farmers and some of the lesser textile nobility of both North and South Carolina invested heavily in the Anderson Motor Company. *Poor's* and *Moody's Industrials*, leading financial publications, contained basic data on the company and estimated that a total of 4,000 cars would be produced that year. The first rating of Anderson stock appeared in *Moody's Industrials* in 1922. Preferred was rated as Ca—"speculative" with weak or very moderate income resources; common was tabbed at Da—"largely hopeless, even from a speculative standpoint." The 1922 edition also states that the Rock Hill plant had an annual potential of 8,000 cars, but would produce only 1,200 a year. The mavens of Wall Street were not enamored with the company. They were issuing warnings that Anderson would be unable to secure adequate capital or battle Northern automakers.

Some two hundred workmen were busy turning out Andersons as fast as they could. Julius F. Brown, who worked in the Anderson plant, recalls how the three-by-ten-foot sheets of twenty-gauge Armco metal from Middletown, Ohio, were cut and fitted to door and body frames made of local ash and oak that had been specially treated. Dupont Rayntite tops were attached to conventional convertibles, but John Anderson took special pride in his "metal" convertible. A curved sheet fit neatly over the rear seat of a five-passenger model and turned it instantly into a snappy three-passenger sports car. According to Brown, Anderson was among the first of the automakers to use bright contrasting colors. The company also continued to turn out "special jobs" just as it had done during the buggy days, and Brown recalled one shipment of Andersons that went to Spain. A handful of workmen who live in Rock Hill still delight in reminiscing about the excellent materials and great care that went into each Anderson, and today Julius Brown still has in his possession a small biscuit tin he cut from Anderson aluminum in the early 1920s. J.G. Anderson bought the best of everything—fine metal, superb upholstery, plate glass windshields and mechanical components bearing names widely respected even today—and the coachwork was superb. Nothing could be finer. Of course, the Anderson Motor Company was essentially an assembly plant. Rock Hill's main contribution was skilled coachwork; everything else—lights, speedometer, horns, tires, engine, electrical circuit, clutch springs and steering wheel—was shipped to the South Carolina city to be fitted onto an Anderson body.[19] That is why a steady flow of capital was essential. Parts had to be purchased from afar and Anderson depended on their prompt arrival so that he could assemble his cars in Rock Hill. Any supply disruption would undermine his operation. If financing dried up, the company's future would be imperiled.

In some ways, the company reached its peak in the spring of 1920. W.C. Starnes of Rock Hill, head "trimmer" in the upholstery department, recalls turning out twenty-two models on several red-letter days. He also remembers that in 1920 the company seemed to be doing well, but after the changeover to a cheaper model—even though more units were built—things "just didn't seem to click."

In April 1920, panic seized the entire auto industry. Because of the amounts dealers were demanding, prospective customers decided to wait until prices dropped. There was, in fact, a buyers' strike during the spring and summer months. Dealers, already overstocked, were plagued by "trade-ins," a perplexing problem that this new industry had not yet solved. Detroit workers were dismissed by the thousands; expansion plans were shelved; and, although 1921 witnessed some revival due to price cuts, there was no real recovery until early in 1922.[20]

The rumble seat of an "incomparable" Anderson convertible was highlighted in this 1920 illustration.

In *The Automobile Industry: The Coming of Age of Capitalism's Favorite Child*, Edward D. Kennedy calls these years "the first crisis." Blaming overpricing and overexpansion, he describes how in September 1920, Henry Ford trimmed prices some $135 to $180 per model. Other producers had to follow his lead. As is well known, Ford also forced dealers to accept shipments they did not want. This crisis forced W.C. Durant from the helm at General Motors. Unable to find a buyer on the market for his huge stock holdings, Durant sold out privately to the Duponts, establishing ties that continued for decades. The industry had hoped to produce 3,000,000 units in 1920 but fell 750,000 short.

Anderson seemed perplexed about the problems facing the industry. He remained slow to grasp the dynamics of automaking and misjudged the market. The reason people in South Carolina were not buying his cars was quite simple: they cost too much. It was true that prices were cut early in 1921 by some $350; but one could still buy a Ford in Rock Hill for one-half to one-fourth the cost of the Anderson. To be sure, it didn't have many of the extras one got with the local product, such as silver fittings, satin-covered rope and twin vanity sets, but Henry Ford's basic black Model T usually got passengers to their destinations. The Ford dealer in Rock Hill advertised these prices (FOB Detroit) in June 1921: chassis, $345; runabout, $370; touring car, $415; coupe, $695; sedan, $760. At approximately the same time, an Anderson ranged in price from $1,650 to $2,550. In 1916 the Rock Hill product cost as much as a Paige, Reo Six or Chalmers Six. By 1920 it was in a price class with Chandler Six, Crawford or Jackson Six. In perhaps more meaningful terms, an Anderson cost less than a Packard ($2,500–$3,200), but more than a Studebaker ($975–$2,750), Nash ($915–$2,190), Oakland ($975–$1,545), Maxwell ($885–$1,335), Essex ($1,045–$1,145) or Chevrolet ($510–$860). Also, this price differential must be considered against the background of severely depressed agriculture. The boll weevil had shredded the cotton crop. These figures show clearly, however, that in the early 1920s Ford was the real competitor of Anderson and all other car manufacturers as well. Ford was selling his basic black product cheaper, and it was readily available—even in Rock Hill.

Yet after selling only 630 cars in 1922, Anderson shipped 1,875 models in 1923. The following year (the last full twelve months of production) 616 units were built. Throughout these months Anderson's "buy at home" campaign increased in intensity. He told of stellar sales in the North and West, pointed frequently to his weekly payroll of $8,000 and warned "what a hole would be left in Rock Hill should the Motor Company be taken away." Anderson even began to publish monthly production and sales figures. These totals were increased somewhat by improving business conditions, but even more by lower prices. Too late, Anderson had grasped the importance of cost over quality.

At his annual sales conference in August 1922—complete with vaudeville, jazz bands and a scheduled radio concert that didn't materialize when the radio failed to cooperate—Anderson unveiled a new smaller Light Aluminum Six. It was greeted with great enthusiasm. Even before the meeting ended some 5,000 models had been ordered. One could buy the new aluminum touring car for $1,195 (FOB Rock Hill). Nevertheless, anyone who wanted just economy would turn to Detroit. At the same time, a Ford touring car was selling for $298 (FOB Detroit). In addition, Henry Ford had developed a weekly purchase plan with which Rock Hill banks cooperated. Local residents could buy his car for as little as $5 per week. Ford was a ferocious competitor who ceded nothing to men like John Gary Anderson.

The Anderson Motor Company was in serious trouble. During the summer of 1923 the board of directors decided to refinance and reduce the

A Model 400-D Anderson Touring Car visits Charleston in 1922.

amount of common stock, pegging total capitalization at $2,162,000, the bulk of this being preferred stock. However, nothing seemed to help. Even the personal appearance of Governor Thomas G. McLeod at a meeting of Greenville stockholders failed to spark recovery. Stockholders approved Anderson's drive to sell $500,000 in preferred stock at 8 percent. They listened sympathetically as he explained that (like all businesses) his had been caught up in a postwar cycle of boom and bust, but they did not come forward to buy the new issue.[21]

Among the factors that doomed the company was a significant defect in the 1923 Aluminum Six's engine. Several hundred of the automobiles suffered from faulty engine blocks. It appeared that many of the blocks were not allowed to age properly before being machined and this resulted in green block warpage in short-term usage. The warpage broke rings, which then caused power loss and oil pumping. This unfortunate development shut down production as Anderson frantically tried to ascertain the cause of the engine's failure. This catastrophe came at the worst possible moment.[22]

The company, locked in a fierce battle with the cheaper Ford, could ill afford the flawed engines. Although every effort was made by manufacturer Continental and Anderson to remedy the situation with new block assemblies and even complete engines, the shutdown had cost the company a fortune in time, prestige and money. John Gary Anderson, a man of his word, supplied new engine designs from Continental, but the damage to his company had already been done. The community, which had known Anderson since his arrival at the train station in 1877, now whispered that something had gone terribly wrong with the automotive wizard of Rock Hill.

In July 1924, the Andersons admitted they had come upon "adverse conditions." That was, of course, an understatement. Nevertheless, though sales were down, they stoutly maintained the company was "thoroughly solvent." To prove this they published a complete financial statement audited by the same New York firm that regularly inspected the books of the city of Rock Hill. It revealed plant and equipment valued at $617,000, an inventory of material on hand estimated at $413,000 (notes owed by the company almost equaled this figure), $242,000 in accounts and notes due the company considered as "good risks" and $5,700 in cash. Summarized, this audit indicated assets of $1,315,118 and liabilities of $494,758. Though at first glance this may appear healthy, one obvious weakness (in retrospect) lay in the assumption that the inventory of a struggling motor company could be assessed at market value. And "good risks" proved to be an oxymoron.

There was another feeble attempt to issue more stock in 1925, but nothing came of it and production gradually ceased. In May of that year all of the holdings of the old buggy company—eight bungalows, a sixty-five-room hotel, two business buildings and three lots—were sold at auction, an obvious attempt to raise money. In July, W.A. Anderson, former vice-president of the Motor Company, left for Florida, drawn by the real estate boom. Stockholders were supposed to meet in August, but a majority failed to appear and the meeting was postponed. The company was in its death throes, and now tax collectors descended on the ill patient, demanding payment in full.

Early in 1926, the Anderson Motor Company filed a protest with the state tax commission, declaring taxes of $58,000 exorbitant. In February, W.B. Wilson, Anderson's general counsel, told reporters that the commission was in no way responsible for the failure of his client. He pointed instead to money lost on war contracts, model changes and refinancing projects. In September 1926, the company and all its assets were sold at auction to trustees of the stockholders for $53,000, the sum set by a court decree. This was really a simple case of foreclosure to secure back taxes; apparently the commission had agreed to a reduction in the tax assessment from $58,000 to $53,000. "And thus," said the *Record* (September 9, 1926), "comes to an end the most ambitious enterprise ever launched in Rock Hill." A company over $800,000 in the black in July 1924 could not pay state and local taxes of $53,000 eighteen months later.[23] The Anderson automobile, as fine as it was, had unexpectedly

John Anderson Gill, the entrepreneur's grandson, inspects his Anderson Coach Car in 1965. This exquisite vehicle was restored, and Gill and the author rode in it in the summer of 2005.

An engine display of a 1919 Anderson Car.

careened off the highway, slamming into a financial thicket. All that was left was wreckage and a bruised John Gary Anderson.

As the reality of the death of the Anderson Car settled in, critics, who had always expressed doubts, were joined by irate stockholders who heaped scorn on Anderson, questioning his management decisions. His *Autobiography* devotes more than one hundred pages to a bitter, rambling indictment of Rock Hill. Although he admits some errors, he takes aim at Rock Hill and its "leaders." Despite what he, his buggies and his automobile had done for that New South community, when *he* needed help none was forthcoming. Anderson lambastes his business contemporaries as men of little vision, men with "a luncheon club flair and cross-road-town's complex." They lacked his willingness to take risks, to stand behind entrepreneurs such as himself.[24]

The sale of his plant to a New York concern, M. Lowenstein, irked Anderson. That textile operation purchased the property for one-tenth of its value. Taxpayers paid for new water lines and granted the new firm, Rock Hill Printing and Finishing Company, tax breaks. Why not do all this for a *local* firm? If a community can go into debt to lure new industry, why not assist industry already operating in its midst?[25]

John Gary Anderson, writing in exile, asked good questions, but he failed to mention the number one factor for his undoing: price competition. His own advertising campaign focused on the source of his destruction—his automobile, despite its beauty, was "a little higher in price." And Henry Ford offered the consumers of the Roaring Twenties a cheaper alternative which they could not afford to pass up, even if they had to abandon a car "made in Dixie." Ford—not Anderson—grasped the stark reality that customers will choose value over quality every time. Anderson, the self-made man who had contributed so much to his adopted hometown of Rock Hill, was a victim of the brutal laws of economics. The market is driven by low prices and consumers, such as those of the 1920s, would yield to entrepreneurs (even those from north of the Mason-Dixon line) who offered them vehicles (in basic black, nonetheless) that could be purchased for a few dollars a week. But let us not minimize the contributions of "hungry visionaries" such as John Gary Anderson, who stood, for a few years, as the South's answer to Henry Ford. By boldly wrestling with Detroit, Anderson had laid the foundation for a New South, a region that would step away from its historic dependency on cotton and dream of its industrial future. That dream would lack the demons of the Old South.

# Conclusion

*Everything my grandfather did had to be first class.*
*John Anderson Gill*

As we have seen, the South was traumatized by its defeat in the Civil War; its leadership shocked and humiliated by its folly; its white people beaten down and demoralized; and its terrain scarred and trampled by invaders from the North. Cities like Columbia and Atlanta were burned. Cotton farmers plowed the charred fields, cursing the helplessness produced by four years of war and twelve more years of failed Reconstruction, an effort that did not succeed in assisting former slaves achieve independence. Friction between black and white often erupted into violence, as when York County's Dr. J. Rufus Bratton, a surgeon by day and a leader of the Ku Klux Klan by night, led vigilantes who vented their anger and frustration on freedmen and freedwomen. In one particularly gruesome episode, Bratton and his followers hanged black Union soldier Jim Williams from a tree in 1871. The lynched body boasted a crude sign that proclaimed "Jim Williams on his big muster."[1]

John Gary Anderson was shaped by the burning aftereffects of the Civil War and failed Reconstruction. He was, as his grandson James Hardin succinctly explained, "hungry." And the automaker was determined to quell the hunger pangs through achievement, placing the hate of the era behind him. Thus, he grew up fast and hard, making his way to a beacon of the New South: Rock Hill. He married well, or, as they say in the South, "up." The Holler family connections allowed him to gain a foothold, and Anderson scrambled up the economic ladder. Furthermore, the political

Three of John Gary Anderson's grandsons pose with their Anderson Cars at Winthrop in 1965: (left to right) James C. Hardin Jr., John Anderson Hardin and John Anderson Gill.

On a snowy day, this 1922 Anderson Car was parked in front of the Anderson Home on Oakland Avenue.

and social rigidity of the Old South was absent in Rock Hill, enabling him to touch the future creatively.

John Gary Anderson was a visionary because he understood that the buggies manufactured by his in-laws would eventually give way to cars. The Rock Hill Plan offered previously unseen economic solutions. He contributed to the development of the city that adopted him. He left his mark on the press, the chamber of commerce, the telephone company, banks and Winthrop University. All of these contributions were useful tools to construct a modern city—a small Atlanta—but his major contribution was the Anderson Car. It symbolically represented the aspirations of a resurrected South that could meet the North on a level economic playing field—and triumph.

The Anderson Automobile Company failed because of engine flaws, defects that damaged its reputation at a key moment. More importantly, the demise of the enterprise was the result of a failure to grasp the realities of pricing. His cars were beautiful luxury automobiles. The craftsmanship was superb. Northing could be finer. But they were too expensive to compete with Henry Ford's mass-produced models. The Detroit manufacturer stressed that "nothing could be cheaper," and consumers rallied to his "basic black" products. Ford promised "a car for the masses…one in every family."[2]

Anderson blamed the city of Rock Hill, his city, for abandoning his company in its hour of need. His nearly nine-hundred-page meandering autobiography documents the pain and anguish of a man—in exile in Florida—who believed that Rock Hill was ungrateful. After all, he had stood as a town father in the early years of the twentieth century. He had been willing to invest in Rock Hill, to contribute to the city's vitality. He had risked much in the critical years of the Progressive era, and he was bitter that his loyalty was shunned by the city's leaders in the mid-1920s. The death of the Anderson Car was caused by economic forces, such as those that had wrecked Landsford Canal. Sometimes, technology bypasses "last year's model." Markets shift; consumers' tastes change. All of the hard work of men such as John Gary Anderson cannot delay change. Things become obsolete. New inventories eclipse old ones. Captains of industry tumble from their heights. But what remains are impressive monuments to zealous men who risked everything to escape hunger. Their legacies are New South cities like Rock Hill, cities that are all-American in stature because of the foundation laid by men like John Gary Anderson.[3]

A 1922 Anderson Touring Car is gracefully displayed near Winthrop's Main Building (Tillman Hall).

# Epilogue

*My mother was May Christine Anderson Hardin. She was the daughter of
Alice Holler Anderson and John Gary Anderson of Rock Hill. He manufactured
buggies and automobiles and made somewhat of a success.*
*John Anderson Hardin,* Life's Been Grand

Upon completion of the main body of this work, I had the pleasure
of visiting John Gary Anderson's last two surviving grandsons, John
Anderson Hardin and John Anderson Gill. As mentioned earlier, Gill
resides in the patriarch's Oakland Avenue home. Etched in a glass pane
above the Queen Anne front door is a graceful letter "A." The porch,
where the automaker sat with his friend David Bancroft Johnson and other
Rock Hill leaders, is shaded by massive elm trees, which date to the early
twentieth century.[1]

Now retired from his insurance business, Gill continues to be an
enthusiastic booster of the town, which his grandfather helped build, and
Winthrop University, which was presided over by Anderson's friend D.B.
Johnson from 1886 to 1928. Rarely does Gill miss a Winthrop baseball
game and, during my summer 2005 visit, we discussed players that I have
taught. John Gill knows them all.[2]

Gill and I rode a golf cart to the home's large garage. It is, of course,
more than a mere garage. Located inside this museum is a 1920 Anderson
Car. The luscious green exterior and beige upholstery is complemented by
polished wooden wheels—nothing could be finer. Gill took pride in cranking
this marvelous vehicle, and we enjoyed driving it around the estate. Atop the
engine was a shiny medallion proclaiming "Anderson."

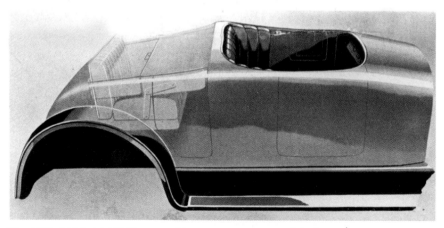

The 1923–24 Model 400-D convertible sports car was one of Anderson's most beautiful creations. These three photographs show the interior and the hideaway back seat.

Even eighty-five years after its manufacture, the 1920 Anderson Car continued to impress with its fine craftsmanship. Fewer than a dozen Anderson automobiles have been preserved, and John Gill's model is one of only two in Rock Hill. But, as we have seen, for a decade—before engine and capital problems, before having the price war with Henry Ford—the Anderson Car made its way boldly down the highway leading to the New South.

My visit with John Anderson Hardin was a cordial one, peppered with laughter. Hardin, like his cousin, has contributed much to the New South city of Rock Hill. His sense of humor is legendary, and his autobiography *Life's Been Grand* chronicles nearly ninety years of service to the town as president of a local savings and loan institution, two terms as mayor and the chairmanship of the United States Savings and Loan League. He has financed churches, businesses and homes, championing the city's development.[3]

John Hardin is a raconteur in the finest meaning of this word. He possesses John Gary Anderson's optimism and gift for detail. Like his namesake, Hardin has been a visionary. He immersed himself in municipal government and guided the city through the 1960s, a tumultuous era for many Southern cities. Rock Hill in the 1960s stumbled, but it did not fall. It progressed economically and now announces at every entryway that there is no room for racism.[4]

Strong and confident men like Anderson and his heirs shape the economic and social landscapes of cities such as Rock Hill. They leave their imprint etched atop institutions such as Winthrop University and city hall. While Anderson's vehicle eventually failed to dominate the automobile industry, it left a lasting legacy and served as far more than just a relic of one man's unsuccessful experiment. The city was able, because of John Gary Anderson's vision, to forsake the temptations of the Old South and to embrace instead the vibrant potential of the New South. That was Anderson's dream—his obsession—from the 1860s and it continues to mold America. When men such as John Gary Anderson stumble, other entrepreneurs, new "hungry visionaries," step forward to try their luck at cranking the engines of the future.

This Ford, priced much cheaper than Anderson's vehicles (and always in black), drives down one of Rock Hill's streets in 1926. Anderson blamed fickle townspeople and unsympathetic bankers for abandoning him in his hour of need.

# Chronology

| | |
|---|---|
| 1860 | South Carolina secedes from the Union. |
| 1861 | John Gary Anderson born in Lawsonville, North Carolina. |
| 1877 | Anderson comes to Rock Hill, South Carolina. |
| 1880 | Anderson works for the Herald newspaper. |
| 1884 | Anderson marries Alice Louetta Holler. |
| 1886 | Holler and Anderson Buggy Company chartered; Genevieve Louetta Anderson born. |
| 1887 | Anderson purchases stock in Standard Cotton Mill; creates string telephone line. |
| 1889 | Carriage business flourishes. |
| 1891–92 | Anderson selected city councilman. Served one term. |
| 1895 | Anderson helps found Rock Hill Telephone Company, dabbles in real estate; Winthrop College relocated to Rock Hill. |
| 1901 | Anderson partners with James Milton Cherry in the buggy company; starts Rock Hill Journal newspaper. |
| 1905–12 | Buggies and carriages built and shipped nationwide. |
| 1906 | Anderson organizes Rock Hill Chamber of Commerce. |
| 1908 | Henry Ford's Model T appears, two years before Anderson's automobile efforts commenced. |
| 1910 | Son John Wesley Anderson helps convert carriage business to automobile manufacturing. |
| 1911–12 | Anderson promotes Rock Hill Plan. |
| 1914 | World War I begins in Europe. |

| | |
|---|---|
| *1916* | *Anderson, president, John Wesley Anderson, vice president, Joseph Anglada, chief engineer of Anderson Motor Company; James B. Duke offers Anderson $1,000,000 to move company to Charlotte, North Carolina.* |
| *1920* | *Thirty-five cars produced a day.* |
| *1921* | *Anderson sells 481 automobiles, down from previous year's total of 1,180.* |
| *1922* | *Anderson Light Aluminum Six unveiled; 5,000 orders received in one day, but Anderson sells only 630 cars.* |
| *1923* | *Anderson ships 1,875 models; defect discovered in Continental engines.* |
| *1924* | *Anderson admits "adverse conditions"; stops production.* |
| *1925* | *Anderson attempts, unsuccessfully, to sell more stock.* |
| *1926* | *Company sold for taxes of $53,000.* |
| *1937* | *Anderson publishes* Autobiography, *dies in Lakeland, Florida.* |

# Notes

## Introduction

1. Gill, interview.
2. Ibid.; *Herald*, February 6, 2005.
3. John Hardin, interview.
4. James Hardin, interview.
5. Ibid.
6. Ibid.

## Hungry Visionary

1. The starting point for the life of John Gary Anderson is his *Autobiography*. This massive nine-hundred-page volume is a reprint of the original 1937 edition and includes extensive material on the automaker and his adopted hometown of Rock Hill, South Carolina. Supplementing the memoirs are the John Gary Anderson Papers housed at Winthrop University's library and the collection found in the York County Library's Caroliniana Room.
2. See J. Edward Lee's *South Carolina In The Civil War* for a study of the devastating effects of the war on the South.
3. Ibid. Lee's book contains a day-after photograph of Columbia, South Carolina, in February 1865. Sherman had seized the city and a catastrophic fire ensued.
4. The best comprehensive study of the war in its entirety remains Shelby Foote's magisterial three-volume work *The Civil War*.
5. Ibid.; see also McPherson, *Battle Cry of Freedom*.

6. James Hardin, interview; Anderson, *Autobiography*; Anderson Papers, Winthrop University.

7. *The Evening Herald*, December 20, 1937; *State*, December 16, 1937; James Hardin, interview.

## Death of a Salesman

1. See obituaries in the *Evening Herald*, December 20, 1937, and the *State*, December 16, 1937; James Hardin (one of Anderson's pallbearers), interview. The Anderson Papers also contain scores of letters from friends and former business associates.

2. James Hardin, John Hardin and John Gill, interviews.

3. James Hardin, interview; Anderson, *Autobiography*. The *Autobiography* clearly documents the importance of the Holler connection; see particularly chapter 28, entitled "The Advent of the Little Shop on Caldwell Street."

4. The *Journal*, September 4, 1901. Anderson's views on temperance are also sprinkled throughout his *Autobiography*. The *Journal* was thoroughly prohibitionist.

5. Anderson, *Autobiography*, 186–98. As Anderson explains in chapter 16 of his *Autobiography*, he had newspaper experience as a youth in North Carolina, but by the time of the founding of the *Journal* he was convinced that Rock Hill's other paper, the *Herald*, was too "wet" on the issue of alcohol.

6. Anderson, *Autobiography*, 470–99. Anderson explains his ties to the entrepreneur James B. Duke, who in 1915 offered Anderson $1 million to move his company to Charlotte. Obviously, Anderson was committed to Rock Hill and, for a time, his business was flourishing in that community. On the issue of Franklin D. Roosevelt's commitment to rural electrification and agricultural reform, one of the best recent sources is Conrad Black's *Franklin Delano Roosevelt*.

7. Interviews with James and John Hardin; see also obituaries and the Anderson Papers for evidence of the outpouring of sympathy that took place after the automaker's demise.

## Music to His Ears

1. Anderson, *Autobiography*, 1–6.

2. Ibid.

3. Ibid.

4. Ibid.

5. James, interview; Anderson, *Autobiography*, 19–28.

6. Anderson, *Autobiography*, 39–43.

## They Call It Rock Hill

1. James, interview; Anderson, *Autobiography*, 19–21.

2. James, interview.

3. Ibid.

4. Lee, *Voices*, 3–7; Mayfield, *Rock Hill Dentistry*, 1–5; Brown, *A City Without Cobwebs*, 7–12; Anderson, *Autobiography*, 9–11.

5. Anderson, *Autobiography*, 116–19.

6. Brown, *A City Without Cobwebs*, 137–39.

7. *Autobiography*, 116–18.

8. Hardy, interview.

9. Anderson, *Autobiography*, 12–16.

10. *Charlotte Observer*, January 22, 1921; Beatty, interview.

11. Anderson, *Autobiography*, 119–25.

12. Ibid., 12–18.

13. Ibid. As Anderson says, "[I] walked in, hung up my hat and coat [and got to work]," 116–18.

## Anderson and Company

1. Beatty, interview; James Hardin, interview.

2. James Hardin, interview.

3. Ibid.; Anderson Papers.

4. Anderson, *Autobiography*, 123–25, 134–43.

5. Ibid., 126–29; Anderson Papers.

6. Anderson, *Autobiography*, 44–50.

7. Ibid., 159–61; Beatty, interview; Anderson Papers.

8. Anderson, *Autobiography*, 159–66.

9. *Evening Herald*, May 13, 1894.

10. Ibid.

11. *State*, May 13, 1894.

12. James Hardin, interview; Brown, *A City Without Cobwebs*, 168.

13. Brown, *A City Without Cobwebs*, 169–72.

## More than a Social Club

1. *Yorkville Enquirer*, October 24, 1888.

2. "Rock Hill History," Winthrop University Library, Rock Hill, 1890.

3. Anderson, *Autobiography*, 208–11; Beatty, interview.

4. *Herald*, September 28, 1892, November 30, 1892; Anderson, *Autobiography*, 170; Brown, *A City Without Cobwebs*, 197; *Herald*, December 10, 1892.

5. Anderson, *Autobiography*, 438; *Herald*, March 20, 1892.

6. Duggan, "Machines, Markets, and Labor," 312; Anderson, *Autobiography*, 450.

7. Anderson, *Autobiography*, 450.

8. Ibid., 452.

9. *City of Rock Hill*, 9, 30.

10. Anderson, *Autobiography*, 455.

11. Ibid., 456.

12. *Herald*, March 20, 1897.

13. *Atlanta Journal*, May 31, 1899; *Mill News*, June 15, 1900; "Rock Hill Buggy Company's Great Success," 347.

14. Anderson Papers.

15. Carlton and Coclanis, "Capital Mobilization and Southern Industry," 91.

16. Brownell, *Urban Ethos*, 48.

17. John Wood, "Reminiscences of Rock Hill," John Wood file.

18. Commercial club presidential address, Anderson Papers, January 15, 1903; *Herald*, January 19, 1903.

19. Brownell, *Urban Ethos*, 48; Anderson Papers.

20. Anderson Papers.

21. Wood, "Reminiscences of Rock Hill," John Wood file.

22. *Record*, October 22, 1906; *Herald*, July 14, 1906.

23. *Record*, May 28, 1921; Anderson, *Autobiography*, 175.

24. Kohn, *Cotton Mills of South Carolina*, 86–89.

25. Anderson Papers; Anderson, *Autobiography*, 550.

## The Rock Hill Plan

1. Beatty, interview; *Charlotte Observer*, August 19, 1995.

2. Eaton, *Growth of Southern Civilization*, 111.

3. Goodwyn, *The Populist Moment*, 197.

4. *Herald*, January 18, 1893.

5. Petty, *The Growth And Distribution of Population in South Carolina*, 231.

6. Snyder, *Cotton Crisis*, 86; Woodward, *Origins of the New South*, 413.

7. *New York Times*, October 3, 1914; Anderson, *Autobiography*, 193–94.

8. Anderson, *Autobiography*, 194; Anderson Papers.

9. *Atlanta Constitution*, January 1, 1913.

10. *Atlanta Constitution*, December 30, 1911; *Atlanta Journal*, February 3, 1912; *Atlanta Constitution*, February 14, 1912.

11. Anderson Papers.

12. Anderson, *Autobiography*, 183; Burts, *Richard Irvine Manning*, 116–17; *Carlton Mill and Town*, 181.

13. Carlton, *Mill and Town*, 181.

14. *Memphis Commercial Appeal*, February 7, 1912; *State*, February 13, 1912; *Atlanta*

*Constitution*, February 14, 1912; *Greenwood Journal*, January 20, 1912; *Savannah News*, February 13, 1912; *New Orleans Picayune*, February 12, 1912.

15. Anderson Papers; *Anderson (SC) Advocate*, January 30, 1912.

16. *New York Times*, October 3, 1914; Petty, *Growth and Distribution*, 231; *New York Times*, October 3, 1914; Anderson Papers.

17. Anderson, *Autobiography*, 192–93.

18. Tindall, *Emergence of the New South*, 33; Anderson Papers.

19. Anderson Papers.

20. *New York Times*, August 28, 1914, September 29, 1914.

21. *New York Times*, August 5, 1914, October 1, 1914; Burts, *Richard Irvine Manning*, 81; *New York Times*, August 29, 1914.

22. *New York Times*, September 24, 1914, October 2, 1914, September 9, 1914, September 22, 1945, September 25, 1914, September 29, 1914.

23. Ibid., September 12, 1914; Burts, *Richard Irvine Manning*, 81; *New York Times*, September 20, 1914.

24. *New York Times*, October 3, 1914, October 16, 1914, September 25, 1914.

25. Ibid., October 2, 1914.

26. Anderson, *Autobiography*, 181.

27. *New York Times*, January 18, 1915.

28. Ibid., January 20, 1915; Anderson Papers.

29. Anderson Papers; Anderson, *Autobiography*, 193.

## "A Little Higher in Price, But…"

1. The best treatment of the dramatic transition from the Gilded Age to the Progressive era is John Morton Blum's *The Progressive Presidents*.

2. Ibid., 21–25.

3. Burns, *The Three Roosevelts*.

4. Blum, *The Progressive Presidents*, 78–84.

5. Evans, interview.

6. Ibid.

7. Anderson, *Autobiography*, 553–58.

8. *Record*, March 10, 1910; *Charlotte Observer*, April 18, 1910.

9. *Charlotte Observer*, April 18, 1910, June 19, 1913; Anderson Papers.

10. Anderson Papers; Anderson, *Autobiography*, 570–77; *Rock Hill Record*, January 10, 1916.

11. *Record*, February 7, 1916; Anderson, *Autobiography*, 463–68; Anderson Papers.

12. *Record*, January 24, 1916; *State*, January 24, 1916.

13. Anderson Papers; Anderson, *Autobiography*, 472–76.

14. *Record*, December 11, 1916; James Hardin, interview; Anderson Papers.

15. *Record,* February 12, 1917.

16. Anderson Papers; Anderson, *Autobiography,* 364–67.

17. *Record,* May 20, 1918, March 28, 1918; Anderson, *Autobiography,* 404–08.

18. *Record,* June 22, 1919; Anderson, *Autobiography,* 394–402.

19. *Record,* November 21, 1919; *State,* January 4, 1920; Anderson Papers.

20. Kennedy, *The Automobile Industry,* 36–42.

21. *Charlotte Observer,* April 4, 1921; *Record,* April 4, 1921, February 19, 1923.

22. Walter Hardin, interview.

23. *Record,* August 24–28, 1922, July 24, 1924, February 11, 1926; Anderson, *Autobiography,* 742–56.

24. Anderson, *Autobiography,* 642–756; Anderson Papers.

25. Anderson, *Autobiography,* 790–806, 586; Anderson Papers.

## Conclusion

1. Evans, interview; *Record,* July 7, 1871.

2. *Time,* March 22, 1941.

3. Echols, interview; *Herald,* July 6, 2005.

## Epilogue

1. Gill, interview. Unfortunately, John C. Hardin, Anderson's oldest grandson and a major source for this book, died in 2003.

2. Ibid.

3. John Hardin, interview.

4. Ibid.

# Bibliography

Any study of John Gary Anderson and his times begins with his *Autobiography*. Like all memoirs, this nearly nine-hundred-page volume is "author-friendly." And it meanders. That said, John Gary Anderson, born "hungry," led a remarkable life, and I found his account of that life to be indispensable.

Interviews add perspective and depth to a book such as this. I conducted more than a dozen with people who knew Anderson and, equally as important, people who know the Catawba region. A list of my interviewees follows.

Manuscript collections, such as the John Gary Anderson Papers at Winthrop University, help define the personality of captains of industry like Anderson. The people entrusted with this useful collection have previously been acknowledged.

As a businessman, Anderson grasped the importance of the media with its advertisements and readerships. Newspapers and magazines covered the rise and fall of the bold entrepreneur. He was "good copy" for the *Rock Hill Evening Herald* and other publications.

Secondary works keep an author from digressing from the basic story. Since this book is about a man, his times, his region and his city, I found sources such as William C. Cooper Jr.'s *The American South: A History* and Ron Chepesiuk's *Winthrop: A Centennial History* to be valuable. These books placed Anderson in his era and helped me understand the contributions one talented person can make to our region.

## Primary Sources
*Interviews*

Beatty, William C., Jr. York, SC, May 22, 2005.
Chepesiuk, Ronald J. Rock Hill, SC, December 8, 1997.
Echols, A. Douglas. Rock Hill, SC, June 15, 2002.
Evans, Ann Y. Fort Mill, SC, June 8, 2004.
Gill, John A. Rock Hill, SC, January 14, 2000.
Hardin, James C., Jr., Lake Wylie, SC, February 16, 2000.
Hardin, John A. Rock Hill, SC, March 16, 2000.
Hardin, Walter A. Rock Hill, SC, January 6, 2000.
Hardy, Jacqueline A. York, SC, February 6, 2001.
James, Al. Landsford, SC, June 6, 2003.
Moore, John Hammond. Columbia, SC, October 10, 2001.
Tindall, D. Leslie. Columbia, SC, May 16, 2001.
Webb, Ross A. Rock Hill, SC, May 4, 2003.

## Manuscripts and Oral Histories.

Anderson, Carrie Jerome. Oral History. Winthrop University Library, Rock Hill.
Anderson, John Gary. Papers. In the possession of John Gill, Rock Hill.
———. Papers. Winthrop University Library, Rock Hill.
Anderson, John Wesley. Papers. Winthrop University Library, Rock Hill.
Gill, Alice Anderson. Oral History. Winthrop University Library, Rock Hill.
Huckle, A.W., file. Caroliniana Room, York County Library, Rock Hill.
Johnston-Anderson. Papers. Winthrop University Library, Rock Hill.
Rock Hill Historical Research Committee file. Caroliniana Room, York County Library, Rock Hill.
Wood, John, File. Carolinana Room, York County Library, Rock Hill.

## Newspapers

*Anderson (SC) Advocate.*
*Atlanta Constitution.*
*Atlanta Journal.*
*Charleston News and Courier.*
*Charlotte Observer.*
*Columbia State.*
*Greenwood (SC) Journal.*

*Memphis Commercial Appeal.*
*New Orleans Picayune.*
*New York Times.*
*Rock Hill Herald / Evening Herald.*
*Rock Hill Holler & Anderson Free Press.*
*Rock Hill Journal.*
*Rock Hill Record.*
*Savannah News.*
*Vicksburg Herald.*
*Yorkville Enquirer.*


## Secondary Sources
### Books

Anderson, John Gary. *Autobiography.* Spartanburg, SC: The Reprint Company, 1997.

Black, Conrad. *Franklin Delano Roosevelt.* Cambridge, MA: Perseus Press, 2003.

Blum, John Morton. *The Progressive Presidents.* Boston: McGraw-Hill, 1989.

Brown, Douglas Summers. *A City Without Cobwebs: A History of Rock Hill, South Carolina.* Columbia: University of South Carolina Press, 1953.

Brownell, Blaine A. *The Urban Ethos In The South, 1920–1930.* Baton Rouge: Louisiana State University Press, 1975.

Burns, James MacGregory. *The Three Roosevelts.* New York: Atlantic Monthly Press, 2001.

Burts, Robert Milton. *Richard Irvine Manning and the Progressive Movement in South Carolina.* Columbia: University of South Carolina Press, 1974.

Carlton, David L. *Mill and Town in South Carolina 1880–1920.* Baton Rouge: Louisiana State University Press, 1982.

Cash, W.J. *The Mind of the South.* 1941. Reprint, New York: Vintage, 1969.

Chandler, Alfred D., Jr., ed. *Giant Enterprise: Ford, General Motors, and the Automobile Industry.* New York: Harcourt, Brace & World, 1964.

Chepesiuk, Ron. *The Scotch-Irish: A History.* Jefferson: McFarland Publishing, 1999.

———. *Winthrop: A Centennial History.* Columbia: R.L. Bryan, 1986.

*City of Rock Hill: The Hub of the Piedmont.* Charlotte, NC: Queen City Printing Co., 1895.

Cooper, William C., Jr. *The American South: A History.* New York: McGraw-Hill, 1996.

Doolittle, James R. *The Romance of the Automobile Industry.* New York: The Klebold Press, 1916.

Eaton, Clement. *The Growth of Southern Civilization, 1790–1860.* New York: Harper & Row, 1961.

Edgar, Walter. *South Carolina: A History.* Columbia: University of South Carolina Press, 1998.

Epstein, Ralph C. *The Automobile Industry: Its Economic and Commercial Development.* 1928. Reprint, New York: Arno Press, 1972.

Flink, James J. *The Automobile Age.* Cambridge, MA: MIT Press, 1988.

Foote, Shelby. *The Civil War.* New York: Harper and Row, 1952–71.

Gaston, Paul M. *The New South Creed: A Study in Mythmaking.* New York: Knopf, 1970.

Georgano, G.N., ed. *The Complete Encyclopedia of Motorcars: 1885 to Present.* New York: E.P. Dutton and Company, 1976.

Goodwyn, Lawrence. *The Populist Moment: A Short History of the Agrarian Revolt in America.* New York: Oxford University Press, 1978.

Grady, Henry W. *The New South and Other Addresses.* New York: Maynard Merrill, 1904.

Hearden, Patrick J. *Independence & Empire: The New South's Cotton Mill Campaign.* Dekalb: Northern Illinois University Press, 1982.

Katz, Harold. *The Decline of Competition in the Automobile Industry, 1920–1940.* New York: Arno Press, 1977.

Kennedy, Edward D. *The Automobile Industry: The Coming of Age of Capitalism's Favorite Child.* New York: Random House, 1944.

Kohn, August. *The Cotton Mills of South Carolina.* Charleston: Daggett Printing Company, 1907.

Lacey, Robert. *Ford: The Man and the Machine.* Boston: Little, Brown & Company, 1986.

Lander, Ernest McPherson, Jr. *A History of South Carolina, 1865–1960.* Chapel Hill: University of North Carolina Press, 1960.

Lee, J. Edward. *South Carolina In The Civil War.* Jefferson, NC: McFarland Publishing, 2000.

———. *Voices From A New South Town.* Charleston: Arcadia Publishing, 1997.

Lewis, David L., and Lawrence Goldstein, eds. *The Automobile and American Culture.* Ann Arbor: University of Michigan Press, 1983.

Mayfield, Addie Stokes. *A History of Dentistry In Rock Hill.* Columbia: R.L. Bryan, 1988.

Maynor, Joe. *Duke Power.* Charlotte, NC: Delmar Press, 1980.

McPherson, James. *Battle Cry of Freedom: The Civil War Era.* New York: MacMillan, 1988.

Oakes, James. *The Ruling Class: A History of American Slaveholders.* New York: Knopf, 1982.

Olney, Martha L. *Buy Now, Pay Later: Advertising, Credit, and Consumer Durables in the 1920s.* Chapel Hill: University of North Carolina Press, 1991.

Petty, Julian J. *The Growth and Distribution of Population in South Carolina.* Columbia: Industrial Development Comm., 1943.

Preston, Howard Lawrence. *Dirt Roads to Dixie: Accessibility and Modernization in the South, 1885–1935*. Knoxville: The University of Tennessee Press, 1991.

Rae, John B. *The American Automobile: A Brief History*. Chicago: University of Chicago Press, 1965.

Seltzer, Lawrence H. *Financial History of the American Automobile Industry*. Boston: Houghton Mifflin, 1928.

Simkins, Francis B. *The Old South and the New: A History, 1820–1947*. New York: Knopf, 1947.

Simpson, William Hays. *Life in Mill Communities*. Clinton, SC: P.C. Press, 1920.

Snowden, Yates, ed. *History of South Carolina*. Chicago: The Lewis Publishing Company, 1920.

Snyder, Robert E. *Cotton Crisis*. Chapel Hill: University of North Carolina Press, 1984.

Tang, Anthony M. *Economic Development in the Southern Piedmont, 1860–1950*. Chapel Hill: University of North Carolina Press, 1958.

Tindall, George B. *The Emergence of the New South: 1913–1945*. Baton Rouge: Louisiana State University Press, 1971.

Tullos, Allen. *Habits of Industry: White Culture and the Transformation of the Carolina Piedmont*. Chapel Hill: University of North Carolina Press, 1989.

Twelve Southerners. *I'll Take My Stand: The South and the Agrarian Tradition*. 1930. Reprint, Baton Rouge: Louisiana State University Press, 1983.

Wagener, John A. *South Carolina: A Home For The Industrious Immigrant*. Charleston: Commissioner of Immigration, 1867.

Wagner, William. *Continental! Its Motors and Its People*. Fallbrook, CA: Aero Publishers, 1983.

Woodward, C. Vann. *Origins of the New South, 1877–1913*. Baton Rouge: Louisiana State University Press, 1951.

Wright, Gavin. *Old South, New South: Revolutions in the Southern Economy Since the Civil War*. New York: Basic Books, 1986.

## Journal and Magazine Articles

Brownell, Blaine A. "A Symbol of Modernity: Attitudes Toward the Automobile in Southern Cities in the 1920s." *American Quarterly* 24 (March 1972): 20–44.

Carlton, David L. "The Piedmont and Waccamaw Regions: An Economic Comparison." *South Carolina Historical Magazine* 88, no. 2 (April 1987): 83–100.

Carlton, David L., and Peter A. Coclanis. "Capital Mobilization and Southern Industry, 1880–1905: The Case of the Carolina Piedmont." *Journal of Economic History* 49, no. 1 (March 1989): 73–94.

Duggan, Edward P. "Machines, Markets, and Labor: The Carriage and Wagon Industry in Late-Nineteenth-Century Cincinnati." *Business History Review* 51, no. 3 (Autumn 1977): 300–25.

Estey, J.A. "Financing the Sale of Automobiles." *American Academy of Political and Social Science* 116 (November 1924): 44–49.

Ford, Lacy K. "Rednecks and Merchants: Economic Development and Social Tensions in the South Carolina Upcountry, 1865–1900." *Journal of American History* 71, no. 2 (September 1984): 294–318.

Gilbert, Percy R. "Anderson: The 'Coachbuilt' Years: 1923–25." *Antique Automobile* 39, no. 2 (March–April 1975): 17–39.

———. "Made in Dixie: A History of the Anderson Motor Co., Rock Hill, S.C." *Antique Automobile* 38, no. 4 (July–August 1974).

Hodges, Henry G. "Financing the Automobile." *American Academy of Political and Social Science* 116 (November 1924): 49–57.

Hunt, Michael H. "Americans in the China Market: Economic Opportunities and Economic Nationalism, 1890s–1931." *Business History Review* 51, no. 3 (Autumn 1977): 277–91.

James, John A. "Financial Underdevelopment in the Postbellum South." *Journal of Interdisciplinary History* 11 (Winter 1981): 443–54.

"John G. Anderson: The Secret of this Man's Success." *Vehicle Dealer: The Spokesman of the Carriage and Associated Trades*, June 15, 1911.

Marx, Thomas G. "The Development of the Franchise Distribution System in the U.S. Automobile Industry." *Business History Review* 59 (Autumn 1985): 465–74.

Moore, John Hammond. "South Carolina's Wonderful Anderson Car." *Smithsonian Journal of History* 1, no. 2 (Summer 1966): 51–66.

Olney, Martha L. "Credit as a Production-Smoothing Device: The Case of Automobiles, 1913–1938." *Journal of Economic History* 49, no. 2 (June 1989): 377–391.

"Price Classification of Motor Cars for 1917." *Scientific American*, January 6, 1917, 30–32.

"Rock Hill '35'." *Horseless Age* 26, no. 6 (August 10, 1910): 200.

"Rock Hill Buggy Company's Great Success." *Exposition* 1, no. 9 (August 1901): 347–48.

*Rock Hill Magazine* 1, no. 14 (December 1914): 17, 21.

"Rock Hill, South Carolina." *Mill News* 6, no. 24 (June 15, 1900).

"Southern Vehicle Association." *Vehicle Dealer: The Spokesman of the Carriage and Associated Trades*, May 15, 1902.

Thompson, Holland. "Effects of Industrialism upon Political and Social Ideas." *American Academy of Political and Social Science* 35, no. 1 (January 1910): 134–42.

Tregoe, J.H. "Standards for Granting Credit." *American Academy of Political and Social Science* 97 (September 1921): 63–66.

Wright, Gavin. "The Strange Career of the New Southern Economic History." *Reviews in American History* 10 (December 1982): 165–80.

Please visit us at
www.historypress.net